Finding

TO MY PARENTS,
JACK AND VERA

Also from Diana Dennis

All I Ever Wanted

Available from Amazon in Kindle format:

amazon.co.uk

amazon.com

Finding a Way

Self-discovery through family research

Diana Dennis
née Charrington

We shall not cease from exploration,
and the end of all our exploring
will be to arrive where we started
and know the place for the first time.

T. S. ELIOT, 'Little Gidding',
The Four Quartets, 1942

TIGER OF THE STRIPE · RICHMOND
MMXXI

First published in 2021 by
Tiger of the Stripe
50 Albert Road
Richmond
Surrey TW10 6DP
United Kingdom

ISBN 978-1-904799-72-6

Typeset in the United Kingdom by
Tiger of the Stripe

Contents

List of Illustrations

INTRODUCTION:
Taking Every Opportunity

A friend made a comment to me not long ago which has stuck in my mind. He told me how proud he was of what I have achieved in life. It pleased me, but it took me by surprise, as I do not consider, in the great scheme of things, that I have achieved much. I grew up as a vicar's daughter, completed four years of nursing training, and worked for two years as an air hostess before marrying a British lawyer in Hong Kong in 1962. Dick Dennis (1926–2007) and I were married for forty-five years. Our family life started in Hong Kong, before we lived for many years in Kent raising our three wonderful boys. I spent my husband's last years with him at our flat in Mayfair until his death in 2007. Since then, I have continued to enjoy the excitement of life in central London, and I have travelled extensively; so perhaps my friend's compliment was not so surprising after all. In expanding on his comment, my friend said something else: 'You take every opportunity coming your way.' I am inclined to agree.

Taking every opportunity was not always possible. As a child I felt somewhat oppressed by the conservative world of my parents, John ('Jack') Charrington (1901–1985) and Vera Sartin (1915–1994), and I could not wait for the more adventurous life which I then enjoyed as a young woman and which led me to Hong Kong and to meeting Dick. The joy of my married life came, inevitably, with its restrictions, but when my husband retired in 1984, I decided to do something with my life and not to fall apart as my mother had done when my father retired fifteen years earlier. Sadly, she lost her identity as a vicar's wife, a role which gave her every opportunity to be outgoing and fun, and she became disengaged from life.

In contrast, I became strongly motivated to live life to the full. I enrolled for A-levels in my forties and gained a place to read English at the University of London's Westfield College. I took A-levels and studied for my degree at the same time as my oldest son. After gaining my BA, I decided to take a break from academia, though I was slightly tempted to do an MPhil in Elizabethan pamphlets, as suggested to me by my tutor in the Development of the English Language. I had done particularly well in this subject. Common sense prevailed, however, and I avoided all those long hours reading about an obscure subject. By then I had developed an interest in the ideas of the Swiss psychologist Carl Jung (1875–1961), and I applied to train as a Jungian analyst, which, perhaps, was harder. It took me six years. I found my extrovert personality not entirely suited to this mode of life, but, once I had got through the training, I enjoyed working with my many patients from 1994 until soon after Dick's death in 2007.

Since my husband died, I have certainly taken every opportunity that has come my way, recovering that sense of adventure I had as a young woman. I have kept myself active and continued a journey of self-discovery which was first developed through my interest in astrology in my thirties and was given a new boost through Jung and my time as a mature student. I even returned to further study, taking an MA at City University in Creative Non-Fiction Writing. The motivation for this was that I was intrigued by Dick's early years in North China in the 1930s. I felt that even though we had been married for forty-five years, there were still mysteries about his life that I wanted to research and write about. My research and my MA led to the publication of my first book, essentially about Dick, published in 2015 and titled *All I Ever Wanted*.

The impetus for this second book came, curiously enough, from the launch of my first. Richard Bond, my late cousin Anthea Charrington's husband, came to the book launch at the Grosvenor Chapel and bought half a dozen copies on the mistaken understanding that it was about the Charringtons. Two years later, at a dinner party, Richard asked the ques-

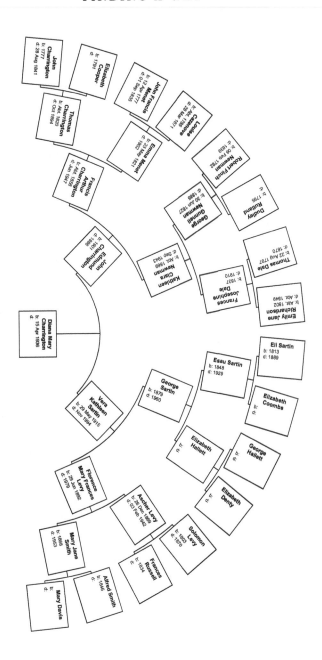

Fan chart for Diana Mary Charrington.

tion, 'Diana, when are you going to write about the Charringtons?' Looking back, he said it in quite a forceful way, perhaps something to do with having been the senior partner of a large London law firm. Anyway, I took the bait, and was glad I had another project to get stuck into as I entered my eighties.

My interest in the Charringtons had been stoked some years ago by the fascinating family tree drawn up by my father's brother, Harold. I still enjoy unrolling this two-foot-long document, as if unravelling an ancient scroll. It shows my family lineage going back to Nicholas Charrington (1530–1591), a farmer who leased Bures Manor, near to where Gatwick Airport is now. It shows the links between my father's branch of the Charringtons and the better-known branches who achieved notoriety and wealth in brewing as well as in the coal and oil industries. Jack and Harold's father, my grandfather, Francis Charrington (1858–1947), was a member of the London Stock Exchange but his share of the family wealth was lost by unlucky investments. The family tree shows his father, Thomas Charrington (1819–1894), was on the 'Coal and Oil side', and that his mother, my great-grandmother Emma Menet (1821–1902), was 'of Huguenot ancestry'. Somewhere on the Menet side, Harold had noted a family connection to the famous Cecil Rhodes (1853–1902). All of this fascinated me.

I also discovered that my mother's family tree was not without interest and intrigue. I made a deliberate effort, therefore, to explore her side, not least because it was rarely spoken about when I was growing up. I am glad to record some of it in this book. I am also delighted to have learnt more about my diverse roots, including my Huguenot ancestry, and to share how I discovered more about it through visiting places associated with the history of the Huguenots in London and France.

It is easy to share family history as the achievements of great men, but I became increasingly curious about the women behind these men and the things they achieved and endured to contribute towards the success of their husbands. Take Emily Richardson (1805–1849), one of my great-great-grandmothers on my father's side of the family. She died at the age of forty-five having given birth to fifteen children. On her death, the newspapers simply described her as her husband's 'beloved wife', but I was determined to uncover more of her story, and I am proud to be sharing it within these pages. Emily, like many women in my family tree, lived in the shadow of her husband, as I had done to a certain extent myself when Dick was alive. I told his story in *All I Ever Wanted;* in telling my story in this book, I have tried to honour the women who, to a greater or lesser extent, have made me the woman I am today.

I admit, however, that it was Emily's husband, my great-great-grandfather Thomas Dale (1797–1870), who most captured my curiosity. The family tree shows how he was the father of Frances Josephine Dale (1837–1910), the mother of my paternal grandmother, Kathleen Clara Newman (1869–1943). Dale's name was more than familiar to me, for as well as the tree compiled by Uncle Harold, I own a portrait of him which has looked down on me for many years in my flat in Mayfair. Before that it was at Island Farm in Biddenden, Kent, where we lived as a family for thirty-four years. For a long time, I did not know anything about him other than the fact that he was a clergyman, but I was hanging his severe portrait in the flat, shortly after we gave up our Kent home in 2004, and I saw on the back a piece of paper attached by Sellotape in my Uncle Harold's handwriting. It said simply: 'Thomas Dale. Dean of Rochester 1870. He died three months after his appointment.' My interest was partly due to discovering another clergyman, like my father, in the family tree. I later discovered how different they were, and of all my ancestors, I have come to admire Thomas Dale most. There is quite a lot about him and the Dales in this book, but I make no apology for the chapters on Thomas and his immediate family being longer than others: he really was a remarkable man.

Richard Bond got me started on my project, but taking it further was helped tremendously by two dear friends: Debby Jones and Hugh Priestley. Debby is a brilliant researcher and I have adapted most of the family history included in this book from her write-up about my ancestry. Hugh accompanied me on two unforgettable trips to France where we explored many of the locations associated with my Huguenot ancestors. I should also mention Steven Saxby who took me to visit the old Huguenot quarter in Spitalfields and several of the churches in the City of London associated with Thomas Dale. Steven also helped me think in more detail about the structure of this book and encouraged me to clarify and expand the sections which deal with my memories and reflections on my past.

This book started as an exploration of my family history, but it soon became much more. For one, it involved me visiting places I never expected to explore, both in London and much further afield. Moreover, it was a journey of self-exploration, for the more I discovered about my ancestors, the more I questioned how their lives had impacted upon their children and their children's children. Inevitably, I was led to question the impact their lives had upon my parents' lives, and, ultimately, upon my own.

Ancestry and history shape who we are, but I also believe our destinies are shaped by the planets. Indeed, I could have told my friend that taking every opportunity comes easily to me as I have Jupiter, the planet of opportunity and self-expansion, prominent in my horoscope. I held back because I knew he was sceptical of astrology, but it has been a long-standing interest of mine since my days in Hong Kong and it informs how I look at myself and others. Together with my interest in Jungian psychology, astrology has informed the journey of self-discovery I have made through exploring my family tree.

It is a journey which has taken me to unexpected places and led me to discover many surprising things, not only about my remarkable family tree but about myself. I finally started writing in Northern California, not long after my eighty-second birthday. It was peaceful there among the Redwoods - seven hundred acres of what was once a ranch and is now a private estate. I was there with Robin Newton, whom I knew in Hong Kong in the sixties when she was only a small girl. Her old school friend, Kelly, had invited her to bring me here on a trip. I had my own little cabin with a gas fire which worked by remote control. It was so cosy, and the surroundings were stunning. Not a sound could be heard. The wild turkeys were silent as they wandered around through the giant trees. I had time to think, remember and plan. I thought of how Thomas Dale succeeded in rising to illustrious heights both academically and within the Church of England, whereas my father, Jack, had not. I reflected on how my family history embraces a few classes, creeds, and cultures: a diverse mix. It was there I was able to make some crucial decisions about how and what to write.

The structure of this book intersperses reflections on my own life with the history of my diverse ancestors, the latter, as mentioned above, adapted from the write-up by Debby. Where they are known to me, I have provided dates of birth and death (in brackets) after the first mention in each chapter of an ancestor or other historical individual. Some of the history chapters are longer than others and perhaps not of equal interest to all readers. I am delighted to mix them with reflections on my own life, as I often think of the lines from T.S. Eliot's 1942 'Little Gidding' section of *The Four Quartets* where he says we shall never cease from exploring and at the end we shall arrive back at where we started 'to know the place for the first time'. These lines somehow describe my journey and are in harmony with my outlook as a Jungian. In exploring my family history - the remarkable Thomas Dale, his no-less remarkable wife Emily, my Huguenot and other diverse ancestors - I have reflected on my own life, not least the environment in which I grew up, namely the contrasting worlds of my parents, Jack and Vera. This research has helped me see how my sense of adventure and ability to take every opportunity has meant that, through my rich and varied life, I have never ceased from finding a way.

CHAPTER I: SARTINS AND LEES
Diverse Roots

I had long been curious about my mother's family as they were hardly talked about when I was growing up. My mother's maiden name was Sartin, and it turns out the Sartins were quite a bunch. Her father, my grandfather, George Sartin (1879–1960), was a quiet man, but the same cannot be said about his forefathers. Debby discovered, from records at the Dorset History Centre, that in 1791 my fourth-great-grandfather, a labourer called William Sartin (b.1768), along with his wife Martha and their young son, my third-great-grandfather, also William Sartin (b.1786), moved from Broadwindsor to Corscombe. This was not a voluntary act, however: the Sartins were forcibly removed from the parish. History does not record exactly why this happened, but it was usually because the family were no longer able to make ends meet and had become a burden on the parish. Under the laws at the time, they were then sent to the parish from which they originally came - Broadwindsor in William's case. There are parallels with the lead character in Thomas Hardy's 1891 novel *Tess of the d'Urbervilles*. Tess's family were also 'moved on' from the parish, following her father's disastrous attempts to connect his Durbeyfield family with the richer d'Urbervilles, a family with noble, French ancestry. Interestingly, the Sartins probably had French Huguenot roots – the name is thought originally to have been Sartain.

The move back to Broadwindsor worked out well initially. Young William grew up, became a stonemason, and married my third-great-grandmother, Ruth Toop (b.1793), who was from Beer Hackett in Dorset. They settled in Broadwindsor and raised their children there, who, in later years, continued to live nearby. One of them was my great-great-grandfather, Eli Sartin (b.1813), whose first trade was a boot- and

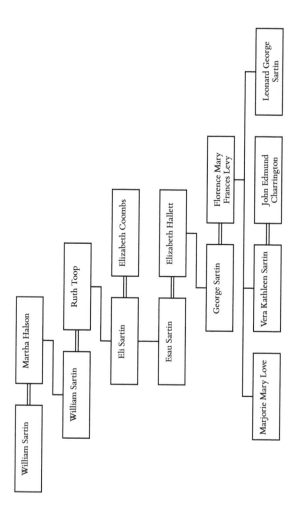

Descendant chart for William Sartin.

George Sartin and Florence Lee, my maternal grandparents, with my cousin Angela.

shoe-mender. Eli first married my great-great-grandmother, Elizabeth Coombs from Halstock. When, in 1849, she died in her thirties, he was left with several young children, including my great-grandfather William Sartin, also known as Esau (1848–1929). Eli soon remarried and had more children with his second wife.

This is where things seem to have gone wrong again for the Sartins. Eli gave up the shoe mending trade, although records do not indicate why. He got work as a labourer and was often in trouble for poaching and trespassing. The *Bridport News* of 12th June 1869 reported, 'Eli Sartin, an elderly man [in his fifties!] was charged with trespassing in search of game on land in the occupation of James Pring in Halstock.' The paper reported not only that the defendant pleaded guilty, but also that he felt justified in his actions. The landowner had caught Eli with a gun on his land at about half past nine on the morning of 13th May. Eli acknowledged he was guilty and said he only did it 'out of want', for he had been out of work for months and had fourteen children. When the Chairman in the court commented that this did not justify him breaking the law, the defendant said he thought it preferable to stealing. The defendant was fined ten shillings and costs. Yet when Eli replied that he had no money, the Chairman altered the penalty to seven days in custody, saying it would be better for his wife and family the shorter the time he was away.

Eli's son William – or Esau – married my great-grandmother, Elizabeth Hallett (1836–1919), in 1869. She was the daughter of my great-great-grandparents George Hallett, an agricultural labourer, and Elizabeth Denty, and she was baptised at the church in Closworth on 11 March 1836. Before marrying Esau, she had had two illegitimate children: Emma Jane Hallett, born 1858 in Yeovil; and Albert Hallett, born 1861 in Sherborne. Emma was in service when, in 1875, aged about seventeen, she was sent to Shepton Mallett Gaol for fourteen days with hard labour for stealing butter from her mistress. She came up before the County Petty Sessions in November that year. The *Western Gazette* reported that she had been working for around eleven months for Mrs Harris of Vagg. One day, when she had been churning butter, her mistress weighed the butter and found it was a pound short. Her mistress asked Emma to open her box, but she refused, saying that she had lost the key. The police were called, and Emma burst into tears and said she had taken the butter but had intended to wash it, not steal it! Albert also got into trouble: he was sent to reform school for a year in 1873, for stealing cocoa. Meanwhile, Esau worked in the glove trade in Yeovil and he and Elizabeth had three children of their own, including my grandfather George.

George married my maternal grandmother, Florence Mary Frances Lee (1892–1979), in Westbury in 1912. I wonder whether my grandmother knew when they married that my grandfather had also had illegitimate children, two daughters then living not far away in Yeovil. She probably did; there was extensive and rather intrusive coverage of the relationship in the *Western Chronicle* in October 1913 when the girls' mother was pursuing George for maintenance. If my mother knew this, the story was certainly not conveyed to me, but then neither was any of the fascinating and troubled history of my maternal grandfather's side of the family, the Sartins.

It turns out that my maternal grandmother's family was also fascinating, albeit for quite different reasons. Debby discovered a great deal of interesting information about my grandmother Florence's parents. Her mother, who I knew as Mary Lee (1868–1953), was born Mary Smith and became Mary Levy (not Lee) upon her marriage in 1891 at St Mark's Church in Bow to a Jewish man, my great-grandfather Ascher Levy (1869–1942).

Mary was born in Bristol, the daughter of my great-great-grandparents, Alfred Smith, a Bristol-born basket maker, and Mary Davis, who was from Monmouthshire. Ascher, who was a brass finisher by trade, was the son of my great-great grandparents Solomon Levy (1803–1870) and Frances Russell (1836–1915). On his mother's side, Ascher descends directly from a long and impressive line of rabbis, including sixth-great-grandfather Hart Lyon (1721–1800), sometime Chief Rabbi of Great Britain and Chief Rabbi of Berlin. Much more is revealed about this line of the family in Chapter 3.

My grandmother Florence went to Halley Street School in Tower Hamlets, but cracks began to appear in her parents' marriage at this time. The family had adopted the name Lee instead of Levy by about 1900 and two of Florence's younger brothers were baptised under that name in Ilford into the Christian faith. Could this be an indication that Mary was uncomfortable about the family into which she had married? A few years later, Mary moved with all the children to Westbury, Wiltshire, where she had spent time as a child before her father took the family to London.

We can only surmise what may have prompted Mary's flight, but a look into Ascher's antecedents and childhood – a riches to rags story - may offer some clues. His parents, my great-great-grandparents, Solomon Levy and Frances Russell married on 19 November 1856. Frances had grown up in nearby Litchfield Street, the daughter of a commission agent, and was described as a needlewoman in the 1851 census. Solomon was thirty-three years older than Frances. I suspect the marriage was an arranged one as Solomon's brother, Isaac, was married to Elizabeth Russell, who was a younger sister of John Russell and thus Frances' aunt. The wedding took place at the bride's home, which was then 17 York Buildings, near the Strand, and it was celebrated by Chief Rabbi Nathan Adler. The witnesses were John Russell, the bride's father, and Matthias Levy, who was Solomon's nephew, born in 1839. He went on to become a famous shorthand writer.

Four sons were born to Frances in the years that followed, the last of whom was my great-grandfather Ascher. When Ascher was born in 1869, his father was working as a kosher butcher, in a shop he ran with his brother Isaac, at 12 West Street, Soho. Jewish families were moving into the area during this period, and it was sometimes described as an outpost of the East End in the West End. Isaac was a leading light in synagogue life and instrumental in the setting up of a new synagogue in Maiden Lane. Records show that Solomon and Isaac's parents were Matthias and Esther Levy, and that Solomon's birth in 1803 took place in Bishopsgate. Tragically, Solomon died when Ascher was only a few months old, leaving Frances in very difficult circumstances. Advertisements were placed that year in the *Jewish Record* by Israel Abrahams, a newspaper proprietor and Liberal Party activist. He referred to the 'poignant distress' being suffered by Fanny Levy, who had been left by her husband's death 'completely unprovided for'. Mr Abrahams was seeking help in placing her in a small business. This obviously worked, as Frances was able to open a confectionery shop. She never remarried, but a further son, Joseph, appeared in 1876. Frances died in a Jewish alms-house in November 1915. She was buried in Stepney.

As for my great-grandmother Mary, her life back in West-bury, after what was clearly a difficult marriage to a man whose troubled family background may have compounded tensions in their relationship, was not without tragedy. It is not clear what became of Ascher immediately after his wife left him, but his fortunes were not great at the end of his life. In 1932, he was at a Salvation Army hostel in Whitechapel Road, Stepney, but the following year, he moved to Rowton House, Fieldgate Street in the City of London. His paths may have crossed with George Orwell, who stayed there while researching his 1933 memoir *Down and Out in Paris in London*. Asher was still there at the outbreak of the Second World War and gave it as his ad-dress when he died on 3 February 1942 at the Northern Hospi-tal. His death was registered by a member of the hospital staff. I wonder whether he knew that his son, Joseph Lee, was killed on 12th March 1915 during the Battle of Neuve Chapelle. Jo-seph was serving with the 1st Battalion Wiltshire Regiment and is buried in La Laiterie Military Cemetery in Belgium, a bit south of Ypres. Amongst Joseph's effects, which were sent home to 21 Fore Street in Westbury, was a photograph of his little niece, my mother's sister Marjorie. He died in the same year that my mother, Mary's granddaughter Vera, was born. I was in my late teens when Mary died in 1953; were it not for Debby's research, I would have known nothing about her earlier life, including that she was once known as Mary Levy.

CHAPTER 2: JACK AND VERA
The Contrasting Worlds of My Parents

It is strange how history repeats itself: my parents, Jack Charrington (1901–1985) and Vera Sartin (1915–1994), barely knew each other when they married; I married a man I had known for only ten weeks. The difference is that I was twenty-six and Dick was thirty-five. He was a man of the world: his first marriage had been annulled and he was a successful lawyer in Hong Kong. I had two careers behind me; whereas my mother had been sent to work in a factory instead of being able to take up the place she was awarded at a grammar school. In 1983, the film *Educating Rita* was released, starring Michael Caine as a university lecturer and Julie Walters, a hairdresser seeking to better herself through becoming a mature student. At the time I was following the path of Julie Walters' character. I was a mature student, aged forty-six, doing a BA in English at West-field College. I felt emotional at the sight of Julie's mother in the film: silent and depressed, sitting at a table in a pub; part of the group, yet not. This was my mother in her later years. Sadly, she had come under the influence of tranquilizers and anti-depressants. She was not bitter, but she gave up in 1969, aged fifty-five, when my father retired from parish life and she was no longer a vicar's wife. She later became alcohol dependent too. Nine years after my father died in 1985, she died in a nursing home. She needed specialist care, which was funded, appropriately, by the Church of England.

I often think that if my mother had been offered half of what came my way, life would have been very different for her. She was born in Westbury, Wiltshire in 1915 into a working-class home. I remember my father having a rather scornful attitude towards my mother's family. He came from a prestigious background, as we shall see in future chapters; but my

Jack and Vera Charrington, my parents.

mother's ancestry was hardly spoken about. It was only with the help of my researcher friend, Debby, that I discovered things about my mother's family history which came as quite a revelation to me. No mention was ever made to me of my Jewish relatives. I am one eighth Jewish and my sons were excited to learn they had Jewish ancestry: 'Only one sixteenth', I told them, but as my niece, Joanna Charrington, said, 'Every little helps.' Her business partner in the music industry is Jewish.

My memories of my maternal grandparents, George Sartin (1879–1960) and Florence Lee (1892–1979), are scant. My mother took me down to the West Country for the birth of my brother, Tony, which took place at Yeovil Maternity Hospital on 9 October 1939. I was three years old. My grandparents lived at 24 Westfield Crescent on a large council housing estate. My grandmother was small and very kind, a nervous kind of person, with little energy. She spent a great deal of time chatting to neighbours. I remember she wore carpet slippers. Grandad was quiet and patient; he worked on his allotment in his spare time. For jobs he worked at the *Western Gazette* and the glove factory for which Yeovil was famous. He had served in the First World War. I remember the outside lavatory at their home and being bathed in the kitchen sink. I remember the chamber pot under the bed upstairs. To phone home we walked down the street to the public phone box, to make our long-distance calls. We would press Button A if connected or Button B if no reply and to get our money back. It was very exciting to get through and talk to someone a long way off, such as my father in London, who remained in London while we visited Somerset for the birth of my brother.

Later, I remember that my mother's sister, my Auntie Marjorie, and her husband Ronald Love, who had just been demobbed from the Royal Air Force, bought a house at 42 Grove Avenue, Yeovil. This was a far cry from 24 Westfield Crescent. It seemed luxurious and I loved the garden, particularly the mauve blossoms of the lilac tree. For my fourth birthday, my aunt gave me a bunch of lilac and a tin of pilchards, my favourite food. My cousin Angela was born the year after and I was shocked when my aunt told me one day, 'You're a dear little girl, and I love you almost as much as my own little girl.' It had never occurred to me that she would love me less. They later moved to Chippenham and Uncle Ron took over his family's grocery business. There was a constant supply of sweets, even though they were rationed during wartime. Sadly, this was not good for my teeth. In those days, there was no fluoride in the water, nor in toothpaste. I was taken to the dentist to have decayed teeth removed and was put under gas. It took me years to be able to go to the dentist without being fearful.

I got the impression the Loves had more money than us: they had a television in 1947, the year of the Royal Wedding of the then Princess Elizabeth to Philip Mountbatten. My mother must have taken me out of school to watch it. The wedding was on 20 November and we drove all the way cross country to watch the great event, from where we were then living in Bosbury in Herefordshire to Chippenham in Wiltshire. It was snowing, and by mistake we found ourselves on the runway of Minchinhampton airfield! It was a scary moment. We were in the middle of Gloucestershire and had no clue where we were. My mother did a sterling job driving, however. She had only recently passed her test after we moved from East London and was very proud that she passed first time in Hereford. The country was alien to her as she had spent her life in towns and her married life so far had been spent in Essex and East London. My father did not join us for this trip, perhaps because he disliked my Aunt Marjorie. He criticised her for being 'too sexy' and blamed this on her eating too much red meat. Aunt Marjorie was none too keen on him in return and said she was thankful I had my mother's personality. The difference between them was partly due to their contrasting personalities, but it was also due to the contrast in the background of my mother Vera's family and the world in which my father Jack was born and raised.

CHAPTER 3 : LEVYS AND RUSSELLS
Rabbis in the Family

The ancestral origins of my maternal grandmother, Florence Mary Lee (1892–1979), lie in Poland, with a distinguished line of rabbis, including my sixth-great-grandfather, Hirschel ben Arye Löb Levin (1721–1800), also known as Hart Lyon. Florence's paternal grandmother, who we encountered in Chapter 1, was Frances Russell (1836–1915), and her parents were John Jacob Russell (b.1799) and Catherine Yetta Lawrence (1796–1881). John's mother was Sarah Levin (b.1779) whose grandparents on the side of her mother, Beila Hirschell (b.1755), were Hart Lyon and Golda Cohen (d.1794).

From Cecil Roth's *History of the Great Synagogue* (first published in 1950) we learn that Hirschel, or Hart, was born in Rzeszow in south-east Poland in 1721, the son of Aryeh Leib Ben Saul and Miriam Ashkenazi. Aryeh went on to become Rabbi of Amsterdam but when Hart was born, he was Rabbi in Rzeszow. Hart studied under his father and at a yeshivah in Glogau (also in Poland). It was here he met his wife Golda, herself the daughter of a notable member of the Jewish community in Glogau. When he was aged around twenty, he accompanied his father to Amsterdam.

Hart arrived in London in 1757, to take up appointment as Rabbi of the Great Synagogue; his reputation had preceded him as a renowned scholar and Hebrew linguist. The Hambro Synagogue also paid some of his salary, apparently a handsome one. At the time, the Seven Years War (1756–1763) between Britain and France was under way and, in one of his early sermons at the Great Synagogue, he reminded his congregation that they were lucky to live in a country 'where Israel is treated with kindness and they enjoy liberty'. There is a portrait of him in the Jewish Museum in London.

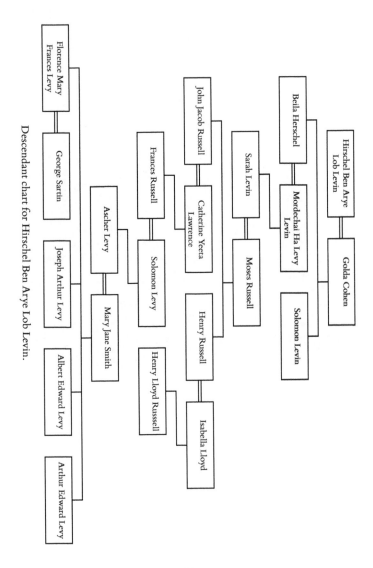

Descendant chart for Hirschel Ben Arye Lob Levin.

Hart Lyon, my sixth-great-grandfather.

Hart was not impressed with the situation he found in London. It is important to note that Jews had only been allowed back into the country a little over a hundred years beforehand, by Oliver Cromwell. Hart was shocked to find there was no scholastic institution for the study of the Talmud, so he set one up in his house. The standard of religious observance was not high. Sources reveal that Jews would: congregate outside the post office on Sabbath mornings to receive their mail and would ask Gentiles to open it; join their Christian neighbours in eating Christmas pudding; play cards at the coffee houses when they should have been studying; attend theatre rather than Jewish places of worship; and that the women wore gowns with a 'shocking décolletage!' 'Heaven knows how weary I am of life here,' Hart cried in a pulpit address in the summer of 1762, 'I cannot bear witnessing any longer all you do in public and in private!'

In 1764, Hart left London with Golda and their children. They went first to Halberstadt, then to Mannheim, before travelling on to Berlin, which became their last resting place. Roth's *History of the Great Synagogue* states that Hart said in London he had money but no Jews, in Mannheim Jews but no money, and in Berlin neither the one nor the other.

Berlin was of course then the capital of the Kingdom of Prussia, and Hart's first years there were under the rule of Frederick the Great (1712–1786). The King tolerated Jews and wanted to encourage a diversity of skills into Prussia. He wrote, in his 1752 Political Testament, these rather chilling words:

> We have too many Jews in the towns. They are needed on the Polish border because in these areas Hebrews alone perform trade. As soon as you get away from the frontiers, Jews become a disadvantage; they form cliques, they get up to all kinds of rascally tricks which are detrimental to Christian burghers and merchants. I have never persecuted anyone from this and any other sect. I think, however, that it would be prudent to pay attention, so that their numbers do not increase.

Frederick the Great was succeeded in 1786 by his nephew, Frederick William II (1744–1797), often described as having been pleasure-loving, indolent, and more interested in the arts. One of the first big changes Hart and Golda would have noticed was the construction of the Brandenberg Gate, his first major project. Under his rule, Jews were also granted full state protection. During his time in Berlin, Hart became a good friend of Jewish philosopher Moses Mendelssohn (1729–1786), and together they wrote a book on Jewish law.

Golda died in 1794 and Hart in 1800, but the family connection with London and England was not severed. One of their sons, Solomon Hirschel (1762-1842), became Chief Rabbi in 1802. A commentator in the *Jewish Chronicle,* calling himself 'Anglo-Judaeus,' described him as being the first Chief Rabbi to have been born in England 'and yet the least English of all'. Solomon was born in London, in Cock and Hoop Yard, Houndsditch. However, he was three years old when he went to Prussia with his parents and he grew up there, before becoming Rabbi of Prenzlau. Roth, in his *Encyclopaedia Judaica* (first published 1971–72), writes that Solomon was a European Rabbi of the old type, with an imperfect knowledge of English. He preached in Yiddish and apparently opposed even mild reform. Solomon is described as tall, with an exceedingly high forehead and a searching eye.

Solomon's older sister was Hart and Golda's daughter, and my fifth-great-grandmother, Beila Hirschel, born in Glogau in about 1755. She married my fifth-great-grandfather Mordechai Ha Levy Levin (b.1751). Mordechai was born in Amsterdam, and both his father and maternal grandfather held the post of Rabbi there. Mordechai himself became Rabbi of Tycocin, which is a small town in north-east Poland. Tycocin was annexed by Prussia in 1795 and its Jewish population completely eradicated by the Nazis by 1941. Before Mordechai's appointment, their daughter Sarah Levin, my fourth-great-grandmother, was born in Königsberg (now Kaliningrad) in 1779.

Sarah Levin married my fourth-great-grandfather Moses Russell in 1798. Their marriage took place at the New Synagogue, which was then in Leadenhall Street in the City of London. Moses's father, my fifth-great-grandfather Michael Russell, was born in Poland but became a merchant and had premises at 110 Leadenhall Street. Some family history researchers believe that the name Russell was originally Hirschell and anglicised, so Sarah and Moses may have been cousins.

Moses was a dealer and commission agent and based himself at Sheerness, as seller of goods and provisions to the Navy during the Napoleonic Wars (1803–1815). He and Sarah had a large family, and Russell Street in Sheerness was named after them. One of their children was Henry Russell (1812–1900), who became famous for his compositions such as *A Life on the Ocean Wave*. After the wars, times became harder, and Moses, described as being a 'fruitseller and slopseller, late of Sheerness,' found himself cooling his heels in Kings Bench Gaol. According to the *London Gazette,* this was pending the hearing of a bankruptcy petition against him. Luckily, things were resolved, and Moses and Sarah and their younger children later settled in Grafton Street, Soho.

Another of Moses and Sarah's children was my third-great-grandfather, John Jacob Russell, who was born in Sheerness in 1799. He was a commission agent, like his father, and then became a solicitor's clerk. He married my third-great-grandmother, Catherine Yetta Lawrence (her father's Hebrew name was Meir according to synagogue records), on 12th December 1827, at the Western Synagogue, which was then at St Alban's Place in the Haymarket (now part of the site of the Carlton Theatre).

My third-great-grandparents, John and Catherine, lived with their family at 16 Dean Street in the St Anne's district of Soho and then moved to nearby Litchfield Street, near Seven Dials. They had one son, Edward, who became a photographer and six daughters, one of whom was my grandmother Frances Russell, whose life I have described in Chapter 1. Again, it astonishes me that I was never told of my Jewish heritage, especially since we had such distinguished rabbis in the family.

CHAPTER 4: MY FATHER
Mr Charrington

At sixteen, when my mother Vera Sartin (1915–1994) met my father Jack Charrington (1901–1985), he was the curate in her small country town in Somerset and she was a member of the congregation. They fell in love ('whatever "in love" means', to quote Prince Charles). She must have seen him as an escape from her narrow life in Yeovil. He was thirty, middle-class and came from a different world to my mother's, but, as he would admit later, he felt more at ease with those of a lower class. There is a photo of him sitting in a deckchair on a beach over which my mother had written 'Mr Charrington'. My mother's parents were in awe of him, and it seems sixteen-year-old Vera looked upon him in the same way as the heroine Elizabeth Bennet views Mr Darcy in Jane Austen's 1813 novel *Pride and Prejudice*. The Charrington and Sartin families must have come to some arrangement: my mother was sent away for two years to lose her West Country accent and learn to be middle class. She was companion to a small girl called Diana Ballantyne, somewhere in Essex. I am named after her. When my mother returned to Yeovil in 1933, the wedding took place at my father's church, Holy Trinity, with the reception at the Half Moon Hotel. The honeymoon was spent in Torquay. They hardly knew each other, but by then she knew how to behave in a middle-class way. She disguised her working-class roots and behaved as her new husband expected. Her performance was impeccable.

My father had an elite education, attending Westminster School, one of the most prestigious private schools in the country. After he died, I came across some of his handwritten notes, penned as he approached seventy. In the notes, he makes it clear that while at Westminster School he felt a misfit. He did not like sport or applying himself to academic work

Jack Charrington, my father.

and writes, 'If I had been born fifty years later, I would have been sent to a school for problem children.' He would clearly have been better suited to a smaller and less academic environment. My father grew up feeling insecure, perhaps due partly to being educated with much wealthier boys. He much preferred the company of lower-class boys outside of school.

Perhaps he also felt insecure due to his family being the poor relations of those Charringtons who ran large and very successful coal and brewing businesses. My paternal grandfather, Francis Charrington (1858–1947), must have had hopes for his future when he married my paternal grandmother, Kathleen Clara Newman (1869–1943). She also came from an affluent family: her father, my great-grandfather George Gunnell Newman (1827–1885) had joined the law firm Freshfields as an articled clerk and had become a partner. His story is told in Chapter 9. The combined prestige of both families meant that Francis and Kathleen's wedding was a grand affair. An article appeared in the *Gentlewoman* on Saturday 27 October 1900. It began:

> The pretty wedding of Kathleen Clara, youngest daughter of the late Mr. G. G. Newman and Mrs. Newman, of Redhill House, Chislehurst, with Francis Arthur, second son of the late Mr. Thomas Charrington and Mrs. Charrington, of Mayfield, Chislehurst, took place on the 17th inst. at the Church of the Annunciation, Chislehurst; the vicar, the Rev. H. Lloyd Russell – with the Rev F. J. Poole (brother-in-law of the bridegroom) officiating. The service was fully choral. The bride – given away by Mr. Dudley Newman – wore ivory satin, the bodice having chiffon and duchesse lace. Her ornaments – a diamond and pearl pendant and gold chain – were from the bridegroom, her bouquet being of lilies of the valley.

I am connected to both officiating clergymen. Frederick John Poole, who in the same year finished his role as Senior Master of Forest School in Walthamstow, was married to my paternal grandfather's sister Ethel. Coincidently however,

Henry Lloyd Russell, vicar of the church where the wedding took place, was related on my mother's side. His father was the same Henry Russell (1812–1900), mentioned in Chapter 3, who composed *A Life on the Ocean Wave*. The bridesmaid – Margaret Russell – was one of the Vicar's daughters. This article carries on, at some length to mention that 220 guests attended and to detail the gifts given by the principal guests to the new couple. A lot of silver was given to the newly-weds: Reverend H. L. Poole and his wife gave a set of fish knives and forks. The page boy, who wore a white sailor-suit, was Dudley Hall, the bride's nephew and the son of her sister, Flora. He was eight at the time of the wedding. Sadly, he was killed in the First World War, having followed one of his older brothers, Reginald, into the Royal Marines.

Francis was around eleven years Kathleen's senior when they married – just short of his forty-second birthday - and his occupation was stated as 'stockjobber'. When the 1901 census was taken, he and Kathleen were visiting his sister, Florence, and her husband, Anthony Henley, who was a surgeon. Kathleen was pregnant with their first child, and my father Jack was born on 13 October that year in Brentwood, Essex and baptised in November at St Thomas of Canterbury's Church, Brentwood. A daughter, Evelyn, followed in January 1903. She too was baptised at St Thomas's, but she died that same month.

By November 1904, the family were living at Fairview, Highfields, Ashtead, and another girl, Cecilia, was born and baptised at St Giles's Church in Ashtead. In 1905, Francis applied from this address for membership of the Stock Exchange, stating that he was in partnership with Percival Brodrick. Later, he had offices at 3 Tokenhouse Buildings in the City of London. Their last child, Harold Francis Charrington, my Uncle Harold, was born in 1910. By 1912, they were at 30 Madeley Road, Ealing, and, according to documents Francis filed most years with the London Stock Exchange, they were still there during the First World War, until they moved within Ealing to 72 Boileau Road and from there to 31 Webster Gardens. By October 1920, the family were living at 22 Montpelier Road, also in Ealing.

At some point in this period, my grandfather Francis was to lose most of his money on the Stock Exchange. The combined impact of this and the First World War was very hard on my grandmother Kathleen. The notes my father wrote approaching his seventies reveal, 'Mother suffered a nervous breakdown. Mercifully, she was only away for six months.' An added pressure was the fact that various relatives and others would stay for long periods of time, including my grandmother's older sister Mary, who never married, and her companion, Nurse Bailey. Susan Williams, who had been my grandmother's nanny, also lived with the family into her eighties. Two other maiden aunts, my paternal grandfather's sisters, Emily and Nell, referred to the house in Montpelier Road as their house, since they had financed it. Aunt Nell, my father recounted, refused to sit on a chair where a man had been sitting, if the cushion was still warm, for fear of falling pregnant. Aunt Emily, at a meeting for the RSPCA, asked if unwanted puppies could be drowned in warm water and not cold. I used to love hearing these stories, which were often repeated, illustrating to me the narrowness of their worlds, but this family environment cannot have been easy for my father as a child and a teenager.

Despite their lack of money, my father's parents employed a cook, housemaid, and a boy who came to sharpen knives and clean shoes on a Saturday. They also had a nanny to care for the children and she lived with them for many years, long after the children were grown up. She must have held the family together, particularly when my grandmother was away in a mental hospital suffering from a nervous breakdown. I remember being taken to visit my father's nanny. She had one leg; the other having been amputated for lack of blood supply. She also had a parrot in a cage which amused us by talking. She was always referred to as 'Nanny' and I never knew her name, that is until Debby discovered it for me recently. She was Charlotte Elizabeth Makeham (1859–1939) and lived with my grandparents until the year she died, although her death itself took place in Bedford where her family originated.

By the 1930s, my grandparent's children had flown the nest: Cecilia, who did not marry, had trained as a teacher; my father had embarked on his vocation with the Church of England; and Harold had graduated from King's College London, trained as a Civil Engineer, and was working for the Air Ministry. Francis and Kathleen moved, with my grandmother's sister Mary, down to Littlehampton and, by the time the Second World War started, they were at Hurst, Fitzalan Road, Littlehampton. The house was named in tribute to the home where Kathleen and Mary grew up, Hurst Place in Bexley. Kathleen died in the autumn of 1943 and Francis on 18 June 1947. He left an estate worth £562, three shillings and eleven pence. Aunt Cecilia, who had been working as a Welfare Officer in the Far East with the South East Asia Command, came home earlier that year. Cecilia was musical, never married, and, unfortunately, had a drink problem in later life. She was never forgiven by my father for selling her part of the family silver in Cyprus.

It cannot have boosted my father's confidence that his younger brother Harold was always Nanny Makeham's favourite and that he was a recognised as a hero. After attending Westminster School and London University, Uncle Harold (known to many as 'Charry') started training as a civil engineer and secured work with the Air Ministry. It was on a work flight to Singapore that he met Betty Green (1918–2014) and it was in Singapore that they married. He was working for the Air Ministry's Works Department in the Middle East when, on 3 February 1939, Harold was on a flight over Palestine and the aircraft he was a passenger on went into an uncontrollable spin in poor weather. The pilot ordered everyone to bale out. Harold, at great risk to himself, helped a colleague, Mr Timbers, who was struggling to get out, held back by the centrifugal force. Harold was seconds away from death. He and Mr Timbers survived but the pilot was killed. On 8 March 1940, Harold was awarded the Empire Gallantry Medal of the Second Division for his actions, but this award was converted into the George Cross later that year. He was presented with his George Cross by King George VI at a ceremony at Buckingham Palace in 1941. He went on to get to have a successful career as a civil engineer before he died in 1976.

My father may have continued to feel inferior to Harold throughout his life, even though his brother was ten years the younger. The George Cross is the highest award given for non-operational gallantry or gallantry not in the presence of an enemy. It somehow distanced him from other people. To me he was a little severe and a man of few words, but then I did not know him that well. He played cricket and went to the local pub. Harold was the opposite to Jack. My father was more approachable; his job was to be welcoming to his congregation. Despite his inward insecurities, throughout his life he maintained that outward, confident persona which I am sure had first attracted my mother to the young curate, Mr Charrington.

CHAPTER 5: THE CHARRINGTONS
More than Coals and Ales

In the Introduction, I described how I had always been curious about the Charringtons, not least because of the impressive family tree compiled by Uncle Harold which I have on a two-foot-long roll or paper. Through the process of writing this book, largely due to Debby's hard work, I was to find out so much more about them, not least some more fascinating religious history. Having assumed my ancestors were mostly Anglicans, except the Huguenots, it was a surprise to find not only Jewish ancestry on my mother's side of the family but Quakers and other Nonconformists on my father's Charrington side.

I knew a bit about my paternal grandfather, Francis Arthur Charrington (1858–1947). He was born on 20 November 1858 in Chislehurst, Kent. His birth was not recorded centrally with the Registry of Births, Marriages and Deaths, but there is a record of his baptism, on 21 December 1858, at St Nicholas's Church in Chislehurst. His parents were Emma Menet (1821–1902) and Thomas Charrington (1819–1894). The records show that when Francis was a small child, the family lived at a house named Mayfield in Chislehurst, where his father was a stalwart of the local church and a patron of the Chislehurst Literary Society. Francis went to the Forest School in Walthamstow, which had been set up with the support of Philip Cazenove, his great-uncle on the Huguenot side of the family. Then, the school had 125 boys; now there are over 1,400 pupils and, until 2015 at least, there was a Cazenove on the board of directors. The family association with the school also lives on in the sense that one of the school's 'houses' is named after Francis's brother-in-law, Reverend F. J. Poole, who, as mentioned in Chapter 3, was one of the officiants at Francis and Kathleen's wedding.

33

Francis had an older brother, Walter Vernet Charrington (1846–1935), four older sisters – Emily Louisa and Emma Helen (neither of whom married), Mary Anne (who married a solicitor, Anthony Foxcroft Nussey), Eleanor (who married F. J. Poole) – and a younger sister, Florence, who married Anthony Alfred Henley, a doctor who also played cricket for Hampshire. Francis also had two younger brothers, Alfred (who died in 1855, aged almost five) and Edmund (an electrical engineer who worked in India where he installed electricity in the palace of the Maharaja of Mysore). Edmund died in 1943. An obituary described Edmund as having an 'outstanding personality and a great charm of manner' and as being 'a warm-hearted friend'. He was buried at St Mary's Church in Oxted. My father, his nephew, was one of the officiating clergymen at his funeral.

Francis's ancestors are also of great interest. Records show that the Charringtons had been in Surrey since about 1620, when Bures Manor came into their possession, but the earliest Charrington ancestor Debby could find much about is my third-great-grandfather Thomas Charrington (1748–1834), who married my third-great-grandmother, Ann Humphrey, on 7 May 1776 at St Bartholomew's Church, Horley, Surrey. Through his grandmother, my fifth-great-grandmother Ann Jordan, Thomas had come into possession of substantial amounts of farmland, which he passed down to his children. Thomas may have been the 'Squire Charrington' mentioned by journalist and politician William Cobbett (1763–1835) in his 1820s publications *Rural Rides*. Cobbett was bemoaning the fact that farmers were now 'gentleman farmers' and – as had happened in the case of the Charringtons – their children were no longer working on the land but had migrated to the City. When my third-great-grandmother Ann died, Thomas married his first cousin Elizabeth Charrington (1750–1789). There is a story to the effect that Thomas's son, my great-great-grandfather John Charrington (1767–1841), used to watch the carts

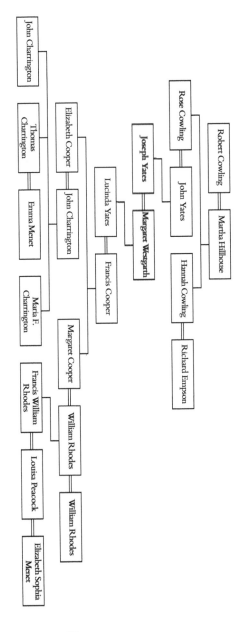

Descendant chart for Robert Cowling.

with fascination as they were loaded with produce before leaving for London.

Thomas and Ann had six children, including John, whose first marriage was to Caroline Hindman at St Matthew's Church, Bethnal Green, on 28 July 1807. He was said to be 'of the parish of St Dunstan' at the time. John and Caroline had five daughters in very quick succession. Sadly, the *London Courier and Evening Gazette* of 21 June 1813 reported that Caroline, wife of John Charrington 'of Stepney Green,' had died at Reigate on 9 June; she was buried at St Bartholomew's in Horley on 16 June. Only a few weeks later, in July, John had their youngest daughter, Jane, baptised at the church of St Dunstan and All Saints in Stepney; she died aged three and was buried in the family plot at St Bartholomew's in August 1816. Another daughter, Caroline, died in her early twenties in Reigate in 1827. The three remaining girls from the first marriage (Emily, Ann Catherine and Charlotte) survived long into adulthood, did not marry, and ended up living in the same household.

Happier times lay ahead for John: his second marriage, to my great-great-grandmother Elizabeth Cooper (1787–1862), took place on 9 May 1817 at the church of St John-at-Hackney. Elizabeth was the daughter of my third-great-grandparents Francis Cooper (b.1748) and Lucinda Yates (b.1755), both born in the City of London. Francis Cooper was born on 21 September 1748 and baptised a few days later at All Hallows-by-the-Tower. His parents were Robert Cooper and Mary Hennell. Robert Cooper was a partner in a mercantile house as well as a wine cooper. Francis and 'Lucy', as she was known, were married at St Martin's Outwich (which was on the corner of Threadneedle Street and Bishopsgate) on 29 October 1776, by licence. The *General Evening Post* reported briefly on the marriage, describing Francis as a wine merchant of Crooked Lane and Lucy as being of Stoke Newington, where her father had died when she was around 12 years of age. Francis later appears in Old Bailey Records: he was fined for not turning up for jury service at the trial of the defendants in what was known as the 1794 Popgun Plot – a conspiracy by three members of the London Corresponding Society to assassinate King George III by means of a poison dart fired from an air gun. The defendants were acquitted of treason eventually because the chief witness against them had died. Francis was not the only potential juror to be fined. Perhaps he was simply too busy to attend the trial. To be a juror, you had to be a person of substance and a property-owner.

Lucy's parents, my fourth-great-grandparents Joseph Yates (b.1716) and Margaret Westgarth (b.1722), were members of the Society of Friends (known as the 'Quakers') and her birth was recorded by the Society, at the Meeting House in Gracechurch Street in the City of London. According to the records, there were three women present at Lucinda's birth at the family home in the City – Elizabeth Childs (the midwife), Alice Hodgson and Sarah Fernandes. Joseph was a wool-stapler, born in Halifax and Margaret was born in Durham, the daughter of my fifth-great-grandparents Thomas and Margaret Westgarth, Durham shopkeepers. Joseph and Margaret had married in 1747, having declared their intentions before the Friends' Meeting at Plaistow. Joseph's parents were my fifth-great-grandparents John Yates and Rose Cowling, who were married at the Friends' Meeting House in Scar Mill Cliff (near Rastrick, West Yorkshire) in 1713. Rose's father, my sixth-great-grandfather Robert Cowling (1663–1719), was a Nonconformist in the true meaning of the phrase: he was imprisoned in 1686, not long after his marriage, for refusing to pay tithes to the Established Church.

Francis and Lucy's daughter, my great-great-grandmother Elizabeth Cooper, was born in 1788 in Hackney. No records of her birth have surfaced yet, but it is interesting to note that some of her older brothers and sisters' births were recorded at the Presbyterian Meeting House in Old Jewry in the City of London. Perhaps this was a compromise, as previous generations of the Cooper family had married according to the rites and ceremonies of the Church of England, in All Hallows-by-the-Tower. It is through Elizabeth Cooper that I have blood relationship with Cecil Rhodes (1853–1902), who had a dominant role in the politics of southern Africa in the 1890s. I already knew that there was a connection by marriage. Elizabeth's daughter-in-law was my great-grandmother, Emma Menet (1821–1902) and her sister, my great-great-aunt Elizabeth Sophia Menet, was the first wife of Cecil's father, the Reverend Francis William Rhodes (b.1807), although she died in 1835 before Cecil was born. However, it was through Debby's research that I discovered a blood connection. Elizabeth Cooper's older sister, Margaret, was Cecil's grandmother. She married William Rhodes, a brickmaker, in 1802 and had several children, including Cecil's father Francis, who, after the death of my great-great aunt, married Louisa Peacock, Cecil's mother. Hence, Cecil Rhodes was my second cousin twice removed.

After my great-great grandparents John Charrington and Elizabeth Cooper were married, they lived in Clapton Square, near Elizabeth's brother Joseph Yates Cooper. John became a coal merchant and he had premises at Lower Shadwell on the Thames. He and Elizabeth went on to have five children of their own: John in 1818, my great-grandfather Thomas in 1819, Elizabeth in 1821, Alfred Philip in 1828 and Maria Frances in 1831. All the children were baptised in the parish church of St John-at-Hackney.

In 1831, Asiatic cholera reached British shores. Its first manifestation was in Jessore, according to Fraser's Magazine, on the 'low and swampy banks of the Ganges'. From there, it spread throughout India, and thence gradually to Russia and to Hamburg, reaching Sunderland in 1831. Shipping from Sunderland was meant to be quarantined on arrival in the Port of London. However, there had already been a couple of confirmed cases of Asiatic cholera in the East End by February

1832. On 4 March, a coal heaver working for John Charrington at Shadwell was, according to the *Lancet,* taken violently ill. His name was Joseph Cook, and he was around 45 years of age in previously good health. He told bystanders that he felt faint and dizzy and had violet abdominal pains. He was taken to a neighbouring pub for brandy and water, but that did not help, and he was then taken to his home at Charles Street, Globe Lane, where he died early the next morning. The parish doctor thought it was cholera and Mr Cook's body was taken to be dissected. The conclusion of the panel of doctors was, almost unanimously, that it was indeed cholera. All this must have been very worrying for my great-great-grandfather. The ships coming from Sunderland were carrying coal and that would have affected his business. Although doctors did not know how to treat the disease, it was being brought home to them just how infectious it was. Luckily, the Charringtons weathered the crisis.

The Charrington family lived in some style in Clapton and had servants. My great-great-grandfather John died on 28 August 1841 at the age of sixty-five. 1841 was a year which had got off to a difficult start; there was a very high tide following freezing weather and in February huge icebergs drifted up the river, doing a lot of damage to the Charrington coal wharf. Several coal barges were also stove in and others were sunk. John's will reveals that money had been 'settled' on him when he married Caroline, his first wife, so a sum had to be paid back to her family trust, but there was still plenty to sustain Elizabeth and the rest of the family. Sadly, their daughter Elizabeth died in 1844, aged 23. Later, my great-great-grandmother Elizabeth died on 10 March 1862, leaving an estate of around £5,000; this would have been a considerable sum in those days, particularly for a widow whose husband had died quite some time before.

My great-grandfather, Thomas Charrington and his brother John followed their father into the coal merchant trade. On

3 July 1845, Thomas married my great-grandmother Emma Menet at St John's Church, Hampstead. She was of Huguenot descent and we shall learn more about her family history, also Nonconformists of course, in Chapters 21 and 23. Thomas and Emma had nine children, including my grandfather Francis Arthur Charrington (1858–1947). The early years of their marriage were spent in Crouch End, London, before they settled in Eltham and then, as mentioned earlier, in Chislehurst, where they bought the large property called Mayfield. Thomas, throughout his life, devoted himself to good works. He was a huge supporter of Anglican church building, not least through serving as treasurer of the East London Church Fund (established in 1880 to support the building of churches in the East End). He died in 1894, and his obituary in the *Globe* reads thus:

> The death is announced, at the age of 75, of one of the most loyal sons of the Church, and a staunch Conservative. Mr. Charrington, who was in the coal trade, was wont to say that as his income was principally derived from the East End, it was his duty to spend a certain proportion of it to the benefit of that portion of the metropolis. He gave, in fact, more than a tithe of his income to religious and philanthropic works. Mr. Charrington was associated with Beresford-Hope, Henry Hoare, Robert Brett and Richard Benyon in initiating the Church Defence Movement. He was a man of few words, but his hand was ever open to support the principles that he advocated. For many years, he had resided at Chislehurst, where he was Canon Murray's churchwarden and right-hand man. Mr. Charrington was an old-fashioned High Churchman.

Thomas left an estate of just over £20,000. According to the *Bromley and District Times,* he left Emma £1,000, as she was otherwise provided for by her marriage settlements, and his plate, pictures, furniture, horses, carriage and household effects. The rest of the money was left in trust in equal shares to his eight children. Emma died on 29 July 1902; it would have been at that point that Mayfield was sold. I was fascinated to discover he had done so much to promote the building of Anglican churches, perhaps compensating for the activities of his and my Nonconformist ancestors on the Charrington side of the family.

CHAPTER 6: ESSEX, HEREFORDSHIRE AND BUCKINGHAMSHIRE
A Clergyman's Daughter

Being at the mercy of the goodwill of rich relations left its mark on my father, Jack Charrington (1901-1985). My memories as I grew up were of always waiting for a legacy from one or another of his wealthy relatives. I remember him being in a foul mood at breakfast if there was nothing in the post except bills. For many years, my parents waited for Cousin Geoffrey to die. He, Geoffrey Gunnell Newman, was born in 1886. He was ordained in 1913 and became chaplain and assistant master at St Edmund's School, Hindhead, where he taught the poet W. H. Auden (1907–1973). Auden wrote, aged 13, that he 'loved him'. It was also at St Edmund's that Auden first met his later lover, the novelist Christopher Isherwood (1904–1986). Geoffrey's sister, Ruth Newman, died in 1956 and left my father a legacy but in trust until Geoffrey died. Cousin Geoffrey did not die until 1970, at the grand age of 84, his longevity being a matter of frustration to my parents.

My father did not necessarily plan on becoming a clergyman in the footsteps of Geoffrey and his famous ancestor, Thomas Dale (1797–1870). On leaving Westminster School, he joined Sun Alliance as a clerk and went on to work for Thomas Cook. With the latter he was sent to Naples and Monte Carlo. It was only after this that he trained as a Church of England priest. He enrolled at Dorchester Missionary College, on the Thames in Oxfordshire. It was there he made two life-long friends, Cecil Chisholm and Lloyd Spawn, who were both to become godfathers to me and my brother Tony. I wonder what he had in mind when enrolling as a student at a missionary college. Did he really plan to work in Africa or China? As it happened, he never travelled abroad again after he was ordained. He was made deacon in Wells Cathedral in December

1928 and priested the following year. He served his first curacy at Holy Trinity, Hendford in Yeovil.

After his curacy in Yeovil, where he met my mother Vera Sartin (1915–1994), my father served further curacies in Goodmayes and Brentwood in Essex. I was born at home, a forceps delivery by the GP, Dr. Dawson. The house in Ongar Road was a newly built semi-detached and it must have been marvellous for my mother that everything was brand new. It was such a contrast to her previous home in Yeovil with its outside lavatory. The walk to St Thomas's Church, where I was baptised at two weeks old, took about ten minutes. A couple of years ago, friends in Mayfair drove me to Ongar Road, Brentwood. It is a very long road, but my mother had written the house number in my baby book, so we were able to find it. There it was, white, pristine, and on the market. The estate agent told us the current owner was a carpet fitter.

We moved from Brentwood to Ilford, where my father was the Vicar of St Alban's Church. The only memories I have of living in Ilford are of our maid Queenie, who, like my father's nanny, also had a wooden leg, and my father sitting with me at the dining table until 3 p.m. as I refused to eat my fish for lunch. I called him 'fathead' and he smacked me. My mother was probably resting as it was shortly before the birth of my brother.

After Ilford, he was Vicar of St Barnabas's Church, Walthamstow from 1942 until 1946. Again, my memories are scant, but I do have some: the air raid shelter in the vicarage; going to Gowan Lea School, aged five; wearing a gas mask; and the Lady Worker of the church, Miss Jiggins, who smocked dresses for me to wear to parties. I also remember Good Friday: no wireless allowed until after 3 p.m. when the three hours service was over in church. Then there is a memory of friends of my parents walking down the street with bandaged heads after they had been bombed out of their home and were coming to stay. There is a delightful drawing of me as a young girl which I have had for many years and realise now that it was sketched by Henry Ernest Hardy (1869–1946) who was one of the three founders of the first male, Franciscan order in the Anglican Communion. His name in religion was Father Andrew and he lived as part of the Society of the Divine Compassion in Plaistow. He must have come to visit my father at the vicarage when he made that little sketch of me. It was from Walthamstow that I was sent to boarding school from the ages of seven to ten, to escape the dangers of the war. I was sent to Herries School in Cookham Dean near Maidenhead. Tony came with me on a visit to our former vicarage in Walthamstow a few years back. He could still recall the smell of the air raid shelter which led off the kitchen and which we used during the Second World War.

In 1946, we moved to Bosbury in Herefordshire. It must have been the first anniversary of VJ Day at which I remember putting up flags across the drive of our large Victorian vicarage. The house was far too big for a family of four, and the days of staff were long gone. Downstairs the butler's pantry, scullery and outer scullery largely went unused; my brother and I were fascinated by the line of bells in the main kitchen that if rung remained unanswered. It was such a grand house but had no electricity. We had oil lamps until Calor Gas was made available. We loved seeing the gas mantles being lit. There was a conservatory off the hall where callers would leave their cards on a silver tray if we were out. There was nothing significant about the dining room and our dull 1930s furniture seemed out of place. The drawing room was more pleasant, and my father's upright piano added to an ambience of tranquillity. My mother had furnished their first home in Brentwood for £400 from Maples on Tottenham Court Road and I imagine she must have gathered quite a few items along the way. My father's decision to move to Herefordshire after the war certainly called upon all her powers of adaptability. She had never lived in the country before. She loved our vicarage,

Father Andrew's drawing of Diana, aged six.

even though it was without electricity and mains water. She persuaded the Church Commissioners to pay for the house to be divided in two, and we had a tenant. She was good at picking up bargains at jumble sales and junk shops. Other people's cast offs were a way of life for her, but she never complained. She wanted the best for me and my brother.

Tony and I both have happy memories of our eight years in Bosbury. We enjoyed the company of the children of local hop farmers. Their parents gave wonderful parties for us. My mother organised games for Tony and me when the two girls from the cottages across the road came for tea on Christmas day, games my family still play at Christmas to this day. 'Tree-Flower-Bird' remains a family favourite to this day.

When I think of what a great job my mother did in making our childhood as good as possible in the post-war years, I am eternally grateful. My mother passed her driving test the first time in Hereford, of which she was extremely proud. My father was not required to take a test, which meant his driving was haphazard at times, to say the least. My parents made sacrifices to ensure Tony and I had the best education available at the time.

When we arrived at Bosbury in 1946, Tony and I attended St Nicholas's School, Colwell, for a year. This was a small private school run by two spinsters, Miss Seeley and Miss Duthie. Each morning we were picked up at the vicarage and driven in the car of a parishioner, Mrs Ruby Bosley, who taught at another school in Colwell. I was never happy there because of home sickness and felt ostracised by the other girls, who were all boarders. I did board there when my parents went on holidays and remember separation anxiety, like I had experienced as a boarder at Herries during the Second World War.

From there Tony went to Cleeve Court Preparatory School in Malvern Wells and on to Lancing College. This was enabled by a kind parishioner, a retired teacher in Coleshill, Miss Williams, and Tony's godmother, Inez Ottley, a clergy widow descended from the Christie family. I went to St Brandon's Boarding School for Clergy Daughters in Clevedon, Somerset. It was quite a long way from Bosbury, but the fees were reduced. My parents drove me to Gloucester station from where I caught the train to Bristol Temple Meads. There was a change at Yatton and then we arrived in the drab, grey town of Clevedon. The sea – or, rather, the Bristol Channel – was brown.

I was not homesick at St Brandon's, unlike a girl who became a life-long friend, Jane Counsell, a farmer's daughter from Somerset. We met on the first day of term in September 1948, aged twelve. We were standing in the gallery outside our dorm and Jane was crying. Five years later we were revising for O-levels together in the Old Gym, stocked up with food from Mrs Counsell: no wonder we both did well, achieving seven good results each. On leaving school we both took up nurses' training, Jane in Bristol and I in London. Only one girl in our year went to university.

When I was back home, my memories of my father point to him liking his own safe space, his own world. We heard repeats of stories from his childhood, about his maiden aunts Emily and Nell, of his love of St Bartholomew's, Brighton, a very high Anglican church. His love of Charles Dickens was apparent to me and Tony, with frequent references to characters in the 1849 novel *David Copperfield*: Mr Micawber who lived his life in the fear of the debtors' prison; and his recital of 'Barkis is willin'', the proposal to Peggotty, when driving the pony and trap in Yarmouth. Uriah Heep was another favourite. My father had a very particular sense of humour.

We moved from Bosbury to Buckinghamshire in 1953, where my father was Priest-in-Charge of Coleshill and Winchmore Hill, connected with the parish of Amersham. In 1960, he became Vicar of North Marston, also in Buckinghamshire. Wherever he worked, he lived in his own world, and it came as a surprise to me whenever he made a remark showing he was aware of certain aspects of the outside world. One example of this is from his time in North Marston. One Sunday, when he returned from evensong, my father expressed annoyance that he had seen 'that bounder Robert Maxwell,' the then owner of the *Mirror* group of newspapers, canvassing for the Labour Party in the Red Lion Pub. Although he had a general dislike of Labour voters, what really seemed to annoy my father was that a well-known figure was impinging on his territory, perhaps another sign of his sense of inferiority.

My parents were distant with each other, rarely showing affection. I was not told the facts of life. One incident has stuck in my memory, which illustrates my *naïveté*. I was fourteen and went swimming in the Ledbury swimming baths, about four miles from Bosbury vicarage. I wanted a lift home and hitchhiked a lift with a lorry driver. My mother's reaction was one of horror: 'Do you want to have a baby?' As I had not had the facts of life explained to me at this stage in my life, I was rather surprised. My mother was strict and swearing was forbidden. I had my mouth washed out with soap and water by her for saying 'damn'. She could be severe at times but wanted the best for her children. I like to reflect on her characteristics of perseverance and persistence, which I have inherited from her, valued during my childhood, and have helped me become the person I am.

CHAPTER 7: ALDERMAN NEWMAN
Very Nearly Lord Mayor of London

The family tree compiled by Uncle Harold told me a lot about the Charringtons, even though I was to find out so much more during my research for this book. The tree told me something about the Dales, but it only gave me a tiny glimpse into another illustrious branch of my family: the Newmans. I knew from the tree that my paternal grandfather, Francis Charrington (1858–1947), had married my grandmother Kathleen Newman (1869–1943), that Kathleen's father was my great-grandfather George Gunnell Newman (1827–1885), and that George had been a partner in the prestigious Freshfields firm of solicitors. However, I discovered so much more, including the extraordinary story of my fourth-great-grandfather William Newman (1725–1802) who came from humble beginnings and very nearly became the Lord Mayor of London.

Debby discovered that my fifth-great-grandparents William and Mary Newman were probably living in Watford when their son, also William, was born in 1725. He was apprenticed as a currier on 23 September 1740 to a Mr John Arnott, Master Currier in London. According to the indenture, William's father had been a maltster in Watford but had died; there is a record of a William Newman having been buried at St Mary's, Watford, in 1736. The fee for the apprenticeship was therefore paid by his mother. This would have been around £20, which would have been a considerable sum in those days. 'Currying' was a vital part of the early leather industry; the name was given to the process of stretching and finishing tanned leather, making it supple and strong for the use of the tanner or cobbler. It involved hard, manual labour. Typically, apprenticeships lasted seven years. According to *City Biography* (a collection of records about personages connected with the City of London and published in 1800), young William 'raised himself by merit and industry, with clean hands.' He became a Master Currier, and the records show that, over the years, he took on many apprentices. He went into partnership with M. John Jarvis, another currier, with premises in Fleet Market. By the 1760s, William had moved to larger premises, with John Jarvis and another currier, Henry Sterry. Their premises were burnt down in a large fire in February 1768, and after that William seems to have set up on his own, at 13 Snow Hill in the City.

William married my fourth-great-grandmother Grace Whitlock (d.1781) on 2 February 1747, in the City, at St Margaret Pattens' Church, Rood Lane. We do not know anything else about Grace, except that she and William produced a large family (at least eight children) and that she died in May 1781, aged fifty-four. She was buried in the Newman family vault at St Mary's Church, Islington. Only a year after Grace died, William married again, on 10 July 1782, to Martha Pryce. They were married at the church of St Mary-the-Virgin, Leyton. Martha was from a family of some note; she was the granddaughter of Daniel Pryce (d.1706), who had been Dean of St Asaph Cathedral. By the time William and Martha married, she was in her early forties; they did not have children together.

In due course, William's sons, Henry and my third-great-grandfather John Newman (b.1754), joined him as curriers, having served their apprenticeships, and their firm became a very well-known leather-cutter and currier business. William divided his time between the City of London and his home on Streatham Common. Perhaps with his sons working in the business and several of his daughters getting married, he found himself with more time on his hands and became involved in public life. He was elected to the Court of Common Council, the main governing body of the City in 1786. The *Kentish Gazette* of 10 February carried a report of the election of aldermen for the ward of Farringdon Without, which had taken place at Christ's Hospital in the Bluecoat Hall. William's

Descendant chart for William Newman.

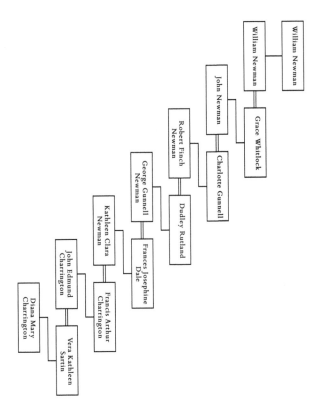

opponent was Josiah Dornford, a cooper. William won by a large majority and then, according to the *Gentleman's Magazine,* addressed the gentlemen of the ward in an elegant speech.

These were turbulent times: the Gordon Riots of 1780 were regarded by many as a potential, dangerous foretaste of the French Revolution; the mental illness of King George III (1738–1820) was beginning to manifest itself. When Pitt the Younger (1759–1806) became Prime Minister in 1783, he initially viewed the revolution in France as something that only concerned the Continent, but he soon began to worry that revolutionaries across the Channel were contacting certain factions in Britain. Against this background, William was elected one of the two Sheriffs of the City of London in 1789, outranked only by the Lord Mayor of London.

As Sheriff, he was involved in in a case against John Frith, who felt he had been unlawfully deprived of his livelihood having been made to resign his commission as an army lieutenant, due to insanity. He appealed against the decisions that had been made against him, but his petitions fell on deaf ears. Then, to draw attention to his plight, he threw a stone at the King's carriage as it travelled towards the State Opening of Parliament on 21 January 1790. Frith was promptly arrested. Reading between the lines, most people were already convinced he was indeed insane, but one of his claims that people thought he was a Messiah may have alarmed the authorities further. William appeared at the Old Bailey to give evidence and he was asked whether he had had any conversation with the prisoner since he had been taken into custody. We can almost hear William's voice from this response:

> Very frequently; I went the second day after he was in Newgate.
> I went entirely out of compassion. I found him a subject of great compassion. He began talking to me very deranged for the first ten minutes. I asked him why he went over to Holland. He said he went eastward, in pursuit of the light. I said, what light? He said, why have you read the scriptures? I said yes, says he, the same light that fell upon St Paul in Damascus. I said, what brought you

back? Why, says he, when I got there, I found the light was in the west as well as in the east... I found him every time in the same way. I frequently found him reading in the Book of Kings and he told me he was learning the art of war and he should come to be a general and should like to understand the art of making war as the ancients did.

He concluded, 'I believe absolutely that he is totally deranged and not in the use of his senses for more than ten minutes together.' John Frith was eventually committed to Bethlem Royal Hospital (commonly known as Bedlam).

William had many friends and allies, one of them being the politician Harvey Christian Combe (1752–1818), who became MP for the City of London in 1796 and Lord Mayor in 1799. The two friends were both members of the Whig Club. The *Kentish Gazette* of 11 December 1792 reported that:

> The proposal by Lord Viscount Galway to drink the Lord Mayor's health at the Whig Club was received with evident disapprobation, whilst the names of Alderman Newman and Alderman Combe were received with the most vociferated approbation.

William was never afraid to express his views, which often went against those of the government. He opposed Britain's war with France which had begun in 1793, and the *Hereford Journal* of 28 January 1795 reports on a motion he proposed in the Court of Common Council:

> That this Court do present a dutiful and loyal address to the Throne, expressive of its firm and steady attachment to his Majesty and family, and of its veneration for and anxious solicitude to preserve our excellent Constitution, as established at the Glorious Revolution and most humbly and earnestly to beseech his Majesty to employ every means he in his wisdom shall judge expedient and consistent with the honour and dignity of the State to terminate the present most destructive and calamitous war, that the blessings of peace may be restored to the country, which this Court is persuaded is essential to its trade, commerce and prosperity.

The motion was eventually carried, after a lengthy and noisy debate about the propriety of the Court addressing the House of Commons in such a manner and an amendment taking out the reference to the Glorious Revolution. William was not best pleased about the amendment and spoke further on this. In the same year, Aldermen Newman and Combe both spoke against the sedition legislation then going through Parliament. Harvey Combe's tenure as a 'Whig Lord Mayor' from 1799 to 1800 was well-received. William then attempted to get elected as Lord Mayor himself but was defeated. In October 1800, he was up against William Staines, who had started his working life as a bricklayer's labourer, was illiterate, rough of manner, and often the butt of jokes from less kindly aldermen. The *Kentish Gazette* of 3 October reported:

> Mr. Newman took great pains to lay his situation before the Livery, and to explain the unhandsome way in which he had been treated for the past four years by what he called 'a designing party' endeavouring to prevent his being chosen, which he attributed to malice, as he had done his duty in every situation he had filled.

The following year, 1801, saw William tantalisingly close to being elected, but he lost out again, this time to Sir John Eamer (1750–1823). Like William, Sir John had come from humble beginnings – in the grocery trade – but he was known as somebody who purchased his way to power and influence. His election was not altogether a popular choice, especially with the Liverymen; Eamer's appointment was met by groans and hisses and shouts of 'Give us a choice. No Eamer. Give us a New Man.' William spoke after his defeat, alluding to the fact that he had grown old but also thanking his fellow citizens for the trust and approbation they had placed in him, an honour that he would feel to the last moment of his life. He went on to say that he regretted that their freedom of choice had been compromised, by the return of another person, in opposition to their free and unbiased choice of him. He could only lament that the Livery of the first commercial city of the world had not the freedom of election. He then bowed and retired, amid much applause. The Court was then dissolved, and the Aldermen were 'elegantly entertained' at the Mansion House. One of the first things Sir John did when he became Lord Mayor was to commission a large and extravagant portrait of himself.

William continued with his duties as alderman. On 29 April 1802, he and the other aldermen joined the Lord Mayor in a procession to mark the proclamation of peace between Her Majesty's Government and France, a war which, of course, William had opposed. The Lord Mayor was mounted on a white horse, belonging to his Majesty; the aldermen rode in carriages. The *Canterbury Journal* reported the following day that, 'Joy beamed in every eye, pleasure illuminated every face, beauty put on her most lovely looks to do honour to peace.'

Alderman Newman died at his home in Streatham on 12 September 1802, in his seventy-eighth year. An article appeared in *St James's Chronicle* on 30 September, quoting from the Roman poet Juvenal, 'Haud facile emergunt quorum virtutibus obstat res angusta domi,' (which can be translated as, 'It is not easy for people to rise out of obscurity when they have to face straitened circumstances at home.' The piece, apparently submitted by 'a friend', explained that in his early years, William's subsistence depended on his labour and due to the circumstances of pecuniary want, his rise was slow. William possessed 'a spirit of undaunted industry' and, after a lapse of years, he reaped the fruits of his labours and acquired a considerable fortune.

William may have missed out on becoming Lord Mayor, not simply because of his political views, but also because, although he had many friends and allies, he did not always endear himself to people. The article also alludes to reports which had been 'industriously circulated' against his private character, which the writer rather charitably hoped had been done in error rather than maliciously, but which meant that the position which should rightfully have been his went to a 'junior alderman':

> Though accommodating in his manners, as inflexible in his integrity, Mr. Newman either knew not or disdained to practice the arts of conciliation. The asperities of his character were not sufficiently smoothed by intercourse with artificial life and many who esteemed the inward man were offended by the exterior. He had many enemies, whom a more intimate acquaintance would have converted into friends.

The *Gentleman's Magazine* of 1802, in a section titled 'Obituary of Remarkable Persons; Bill of Mortality,' had this to say:

> Alderman Newman had a vigorous, sound understanding, had read much and was very highly esteemed by persons in a rank in life very different from his own. But reading alone, when not directed into a right course by early education, is sometimes a disadvantage. The possessor of knowledge by his own acquirement, partially and perhaps superficially, is apt to estimate it too highly and claim too much merit for the attainment. The Alderman was most distinguished as a family man. He was an affectionate husband, a tender and indulgent father to a numerous family whom he lived to see respectably settled in the world. Under an outward roughness of disposition, he possessed a tender and mild disposition and was most valued where he was most intimately known.

The *Morning Post* of 1 October 1802 expanded on William's attempts to halt the war with the French, explaining that although his attempt failed 'for making it, his name should be cherished with grateful recollection by every true friend to his country'. It finished by saying that he had left a considerable property to be enjoyed by his numerous and respectable family.

William was buried alongside his first wife, my fourth-great-grandmother Grace, and two of their daughters, Sarah, who died aged fifteen, and Mary Budgen, who died at around twenty-five years of age, in the family vault at St

Mary's, Islington. His second wife, Martha, died in Watford in 1809. I was so delighted to discover the story of another ancestor who came from such humble beginnings but became such a notable personality. I doubt he would ever have imagined being so involved with politics in the heart of London. Looking back on my younger years, I would never have imagined I too would be involved in politics, albeit not in the City of London but in the neighbouring City of Westminster.

CHAPTER 8 : NURSE AND AIRHOSTESS
The Beginning of my Adventures

I started my four-year nursing training in February 1955 at the Middlesex Hospital in Central London. There were times when it was very tough, and I wanted to give up. I passed the interview with Matron Marriott, and with my seven O-levels I had no problem with the academic side, but the discipline and long hours got me down. We worked a forty-eight-hour week. During our first year we went on duty at 7:30 a.m. On the maid's day off, a junior was required to sweep the ward floor. Before we did so, we had to sprinkle tea leaves on the floor to prevent dust flying about. On days when the roster dictated, my day was broken-up and I would go off duty at 11.30 a.m. but return for the rest of the shift between 4 p.m. and 8 p.m.

There was an underground passage connecting the nurses' home with the hospital. We had to be in at night by 10:30 p.m., but we had one late pass a week to stay out until midnight. There were many times I raced through that passage when I had seen a night sister on patrol. I was breaking the rules by being out late without a pass and did not want to be sent to Matron again. Another thing that sticks in my mind is being sent to Matron twice for wearing lipstick. It seems archaic now to recall that my friend Mary Nesfield was seen by Matron outside the nurses' home, John Astor House, wearing trousers and that Matron Marriot questioned this. Mary explained that she wore trousers for a practical reason - her medical student boyfriend had a motor bike. This revelation was a complete shock to Matron.

I often say that I survived the four years but, looking back, I did enjoy the nursing and met some wonderful people on those wards, patients, and staff alike. One incident I remember is when I had my month's salary stolen from my room in the nurses' home. I went on duty to Queen Alexandra women's medical ward and was attending to a patient called Connie. She could be difficult and cantankerous, but when she asked me why I was looking 'down in the mouth', I started to cry when I told her of the theft. Before I went off duty, Connie had organised a whip-round from all twenty patients on the ward. When she handed it to me, I was overcome with emotion.

Two highlights of my time during training were the holidays I took to San Sebastian in Spain, the first with my nursing friend from the Middlesex, Mary Nesfield. Mary's mother was Peruvian and lived in North Wales. One year she attended the National Eisteddfod, the cultural festival, and made friends with a Spanish group of musicians. The keyboard player was Pedro Ugalde and they exchanged addresses. Mary and I wrote to Pedro and asked him to find us somewhere to stay in Spain. He responded at once.

Our accommodation was the flat above the Ugalde family home, in an old-fashioned block in a quiet part of the town. We were invited to join the family for meals from the time of our arrival. Senora Ugalde ran a furniture shop and was out all day. The three daughters were all living at home but occupied at school. Pedro finished work in the local government offices at midday and would meet us and take us for lunch. We were shown the sights of beautiful San Sebastian every day. We enjoyed the delicious churros dipped in hot chocolate sauce and other local specialties.

We were taken to a bullfight on the Sunday which was hugely exciting, especially the music and the rituals before the fight began. The atmosphere was electrifying, and it took away from the fact that we were witnessing a very cruel sport, which is banned today in its original form. The week in the Basque country was wonderful and I think Mary and I both had a sense of freedom which was new to us. We spoke our schoolgirl French as neither of us knew Spanish. We were away from English reserve.

In my fourth year of training, two of my close friends left the Middlesex to get married and, in a rash moment when on night duty, I accepted an invitation to go to Belfast to do midwifery. I was at 'lunch' at 1 a.m. in York House, the night nurses' home in Berners Street, and a girl in my set, Helen-Barbara Wilson, said, 'Why don't you come to Belfast?' In a weakened state of mind (night duty could do this to the psyche), I agreed. So it was that I flew over to Northern Ireland for the next nine months.

Belfast was a shock to the system. Everyone was so friendly. I took this as nosiness at first as I had been used to English restraint my entire life – in vicarages with parents who did not show emotion, boarding school, and a London teaching hospital. Although I had experienced and loved the more outgoing Latin temperament in Spain, I was taken by surprise in Northern Ireland until I got used to it. I experienced lack of reserve in other people but remained buttoned up myself. I was viewed as an oddity with my strange English accent and was teased but not unkindly. I was invited to several homes of other trainee midwives. After I had realised that they were being friendly, I relaxed, made friends, and enjoyed the hospitality of the Northern Irish and their sense of fun.

This was 1959 and the first question anyone asked was, 'Which foot do you kick with?' This was before 'the Troubles' and I learned to recognise a Catholic from a Protestant, particularly if the latter had been 'saved'. Usually, their strict form of Protestantism meant no make-up and no alcohol. The nurses' home, Bostock House, was in the Falls Road, later to become one of the most dangerous areas in Belfast with sectarian fighting. The accent in the Falls Road is very strong and the patients in the Royal Maternity Hospital had equal difficulties in understanding me. I walked into the ward to ask if anyone wanted a bed pan and they all looked at me blankly. The only thing for me to do was to develop a Falls Road accent. We got on famously after that.

My days with BOAC.

Many of the women who came in to give birth, both Catholic and Protestant, had very large families of up to ten children. The discipline of nursing and midwifery training was tough, but it stood me in good stead for the future. I did not really enjoy midwifery though: there was not the same intimacy as between patient and nurse; the baby came between us. In the meantime, I lost my heart to a charming Irish doctor, but I decided to end the relationship after nine months and, instead of going on the district to deliver babies, I went back to London. Travel was on the cards. I wanted some excitement.

I also had a second trip to Spain at the invitation of Pedro. I loved my second trip there so much that I even considered a job offer I received from an Arabian ambassador whom I met on the beach. He asked me to come and see his wife with a view to teaching English to his children. I enjoyed the heady atmosphere of Spain, but I was quickly brought back down to earth when my mother wrote to tell me I had a second interview for BOAC the following week. When I said I might not return, she was sufficiently concerned to ring me. 'Come back at once,' she said. 'I don't mind whether he is an ambassador or not.' Pedro was sad to see me go and accompanied me to the Spanish border at Hendaye, where I picked up the train to Paris. Pedro asked me to repeat after him 'viens avec moi' as he wanted to keep the memory of me asking him to 'come with me'. Years later, Dick and I were with our three small boys on holiday. We disembarked from the ferry at Bilbao in our car and met Pedro for lunch. He was as delightful as ever, and I took a back seat as he and Dick both chatted together in fluent French.

I had a great desire to travel, so as soon as I had completed my four-year training in London and Belfast, I applied to BOAC, the national airline. Sister Fowler, Senior Tutor at the Middlesex Hospital London, made it clear that she strongly disapproved of newly trained nurses using their qualification to 'go on a buggy ride round the world'. We were expected to stay on a year after getting the qualification as State Registered Nurse, otherwise we would not be awarded the Middlesex Hospital badge. This was 1960 and I had no desire to please Sister Fowler, so I continued to pursue the opportunity to work for BOAC.

'Better on a Camel' was one of the less flattering interpretations of BOAC, but the letters stood for British Oversea Airways Corporation. The flights were all long-haul. The other national airline, British European Airways, was for short haul. Later they merged and became British Airways. It was the desire of many girls between the ages of 22-28, and between 5ft 2 and 5ft 7 inches, to become flight stewardesses. The airline liked nurses, and if you spoke a language all the better. I had schoolgirl French with a failed O-level, but I announced over the tannoy 'the crew members speak French', and managed to say 'Les membres de l'équipage parlent français.'

Applicants had to be single. I survived the two interviews and the not so stringent medical. I was short sighted and memorised the sight-reading chart as far as I could when the doctor left the room for a minute or two. Despite that, I failed the eye test but promised the doctor I was having contact lenses fitted at Moorfields Eye hospital the following week. He liked nurses, so I was in. My mother had never been abroad, let alone flown in an aeroplane. She drove me to Heathrow to have my uniform measured after I had passed the medical and looked disapprovingly at two girls from Belfast who had also come to be measured, 'Far too much eye make-up,' she said.

The six-weeks training school was tough. We were bullied. The boss did not like nurses. 'They are arrogant', he said. However, the great day came when we were let loose on passengers. After the rigours of the training school, it felt like freedom. My mother was very proud of me. I was soon to discover, however, on my first flight, that I had misjudged using contact lenses. When the passengers were permitted to start smoking, I was forced to remove the lenses as they were smoke intolerant. I somehow managed, but wearing glasses was not allowed. Once in New York airport (Idlewild, before it became JFK) I found myself on the wrong aircraft. I asked where I was going, and it was not Kingston, Jamaica but Boston, Massachusetts. They laughed and I made a hasty retreat. My supernumerary trip after training was to New York and I fell in love with the place. We went to Basin Street East where Peggy Lee was singing. I put seeing two Peggy Lees down to my contact lenses, not admitting to myself it could have been the effect of the two dry martinis I was enjoying with a crew member. *Breakfast at Tiffany's,* the 1961 movie, had just been released with the wonderfully romantic 'Moon River' sung by Audrey Hepburn, its star. I shopped at Bloomingdale's and Macey's. My first 'room party' at the Shelton Towers Hotel with cabin crew was great fun. I arrived back just before Christmas and my parents came to meet me. I was 24 and beginning a new, adventurous time in my life.

CHAPTER 9: MORE NEWMANS
Lawyers in the Family

One of the wonderful things about discovering one's ancestry is making the connections between the past and the present. Somehow mere names from history can be imagined as having personalities not unlike people alive today. Consider the three generations of Newman males I describe in this chapter. They were three family-men who enjoyed great success: my third-great-grandfather John Newman (1754–1808), my great-great-grandfather Robert Finch Newman (1792–1839), and my great-grandfather George Gunnell Newman (1827–1885). Like my three sons, the first ran a business and the other two were lawyers. Also, consider the connections to family members, albeit generations ago, who were married in my own church of St George, Hanover Square. Did not these ancient relatives, who walked the same streets we walk today, have similar hopes and dreams, worries and challenges, achievements and joys, as those we experience? We cannot know, but we can imagine, and it must be true that some of their qualities were passed down to us. For these reasons, are we not compelled to discover more about our ancestors and how their lives might have influenced our own?

The obituaries of my fourth-great-grandfather, William Newman (1725–1802), whose extraordinary story we recalled in Chapter 7, all mention his numerous and respectable family. He fathered eight children, but the one who concerns us most is my third-great-grandfather John Newman. He was born on 7 January 1754 in Snow Hill and baptised at St Sepulchre-without-Newgate in the City of London, a church just around the corner from their family home. I have visited this church myself for a wonderful piano concerto with my friend Shu-Wei Tseng as the soloist. I also visited with Steven Saxby on our tour of churches associated with Thomas Dale. On both occasions, I visited the pub next to the church which is on part of the site of the old Newgate Prison.

When he was fourteen, John was apprenticed to Sylvanus Hall on 2 August 1768, at the Curriers' Hall in the City of London. The young apprentice may have been impressed both by the inscription in the Court Room, above the Master's Chair, attesting to the fact that the hall was built and glassed in 1670, and by the portrait of James I, who gave the first certificate of incorporation to the Curriers' Company.

Sylvanus Hall, to whom John was apprenticed, was a Yorkshireman by birth who, after some years, diversified from being a leather cutter and currier into carpentry and built, among other things, the Cordwainers' Hall. Sylvanus became a very wealthy man, and he and John became friends. Sylvanus owned properties in Paternoster Row. The year after John's apprenticeship ceremony, Sylvanus married Anne Gunnell. On 5 June 1779, John married Anne's sister, my third-great-grandmother Charlotte Gunnell (1755–1827). Charlotte was born in 1755 and baptised on 26 November that year at St Paul's Church in Covent Garden. She and John married at the church of St John the Evangelist in Smith Square, with their respective fathers as witnesses.

The Gunnell sisters were the daughters of my fourth-great-grandparents Robert Gunnell (d.1794) and Ann Rozea (1723–1795). Robert Gunnell had a cap-maker's shop in Chandos Street, Marylebone, and he was also a Clerk at the House of Commons, a position he held from 1754. With Lord North, Robert helped to compile the tax legislation that would lead to the American War of Independence. Ann Rozea was from a French Huguenot family. There is a note in the history of St George's Church, Hanover Square, to this effect about their wedding, which took place on 11 August 1745:

> Robert Gunnell Esq, gentleman, of James Street Mayfair, a principal Clerk of the House of Commons, married the beautiful Anne Rozea, a French Huguenot, of Duke's Court, Royal Mews. After the wedding, they had a reception in Marylebone at which

the bride's brother, Jassintour Rozea, well-known master chef to Charles Seymour, 6th Duke of Somerset, provided a luncheon for fifty-five guests.

In 1778, Robert Gunnell bought 8 Paternoster Row from his son-in-law, Sylvanus Hall. The original idea was that it would be an investment property for one of their sons, but he did not use it much, as he lived in Margate. Instead, Robert and Ann used it to entertain their friends, for literary gatherings. Johann Sebastian Bach is known to have attended, along with a poet called Jane Timbury. Ann was said to attend these gatherings dressed in an exquisite mantua and an ornate jubilee hat and she would recite French poetry. The Gunnell children would have been brought up in the family home, which was in Millbank Street. 8 Paternoster Row was sold in 1794, when Robert died.

Charlotte and John Newman set up home in Skinner Street in the City of London. All their children were baptised at St Sepulchre's, as was their father. John, like his father, Alderman Newman, was elected to office in the City of London and served as a Common Councillor alongside his brother-in-law Sylvanus Hall. John set up in his business with his younger brother, Henry Newman, who was also married with a young family. They took on John's eldest son William, then aged around fifteen, as an apprentice in 1798. All seemed to be going well.

Ten years later, newspapers reported that John died during the afternoon of Saturday 1 October 1808 'at his house in Hampstead'. He was buried in the family vault at St Mary's, Upper Street, Islington. On Monday 19 December 1808, the *Morning Advertiser* carried an advertisement for the sale of the household furniture:

The modern household furniture includes…a brilliant toned portable grand piano, a drawing room suite in rich chintz pattern cotton, consisting of three lofty curtains, a sofa, eighteen chairs and tables, two cellaret sideboards, a long set of dining tables and 12 dining room chairs, four poster and French bedsteads with suitable hangings, prime beds and beddings, wardrobes, drawers, carpets, fenders and fire irons.

After John's death, business affairs seem to have taken a rapid downward turn at the Skinner Street curriers. William, John's son, the young apprentice, left for Portugal. John's other sons bypassed the family business altogether. Henry Newman, John's brother, was adjudicated bankrupt in 1812 and died the year afterwards, leaving his wife, Mary Ann, with a large, young family.

John's death, according to some family commentators, was an accident, but there is no tangible evidence to suggest this. The furniture mentioned overleaf must have belonged to Skinner Street, but the family then seem to have concentrated in Hampstead for a while. Charlotte, John's widow, eventually went to live with one of their daughters, Grace, in Ash, near Sandwich, Kent, and she died there in 1827 aged 72; she is buried there in the graveyard of at St Nicholas's Church

John and Charlotte's son, my great-great grandfather Robert Finch Newham, was born on 6 February 1792 and baptised, like all his siblings, at St Sepulchre's. He became a successful solicitor after he was articled in 1809 to William Bovill in the firm Bovill and Tustin, New Bridge Street, Blackfriars. The firm seemed to specialise in representing people who were up before the bankruptcy courts.

When Robert's uncle Samuel died in 1819, he left him the lease of his house at 4 Sion College Gardens in the City of London, as well as his law books and histories of London. Robert also took over Samuel's position as Comptroller of the Bridge House Estates. This was, and still is, a charitable trust set up in the 13th Century to maintain London Bridge and, subsequently, other bridges over the Thames. Sylvanus Hall had also done work for the Estate and one of Robert's older brothers, John Newman, was the Architect and Surveyor for the Bridge House Estates.

On 8 November 1822, Robert married my great-great grandmother Dudley Rutland at All Saints Church in Writtle, Essex. Dudley was the daughter of my third-great-grandparents Joshua Rutland and Anne Lush. Joshua and Anne were married in 1788 at St James's Church, Westminster. Joshua's parish was said to be St George, Hanover Square, another link with my parish today. His family owned substantial estates in Essex. Anne came originally from Banbury in Oxfordshire and in fact Dudley and some of her brothers and sisters were born in Henley on Thames. Joshua was parish overseer in Henley at around the time of Dudley's birth.

Robert and Dudley began married life at Samuel's old house in 4 Sion College Gardens. Children began to arrive, seven in total, between 1823 and 1833. The family then moved to Artillery Place in Islington and then to Highbury Grove. Sadly, just before Christmas 1826, tragedy visited the Newman family when Robert's older brother, William, took his own life. *The Times* stated that Mr Newman was:

> a man of tolerably extensive dealings but an inveterate speculator and that he had suffered latterly some very severe losses, which he had not the philosophy to bear up against and was imprudent enough to endeavour to make them good, by an act which he doubtless intended as a temporary resource, in the hope that he could retrieve his circumstances.

Sadly, Robert was implicated in his brother's loss of funds on the stock market. It seems that Robert had given William some money to invest on behalf of Bridge House Estates. That was lost too. The *Devizes and Wiltshire Gazette* reported in May 1827 that 'the Court of Common Council have decided that Robert Finch Newman, Comptroller of Bridge House Estates, must make good in some way or other £3,500, misapplied by his brother, a stockbroker, whom he employed to invest it in the Funds.' The Court emphasised that no blame should be attached to Robert, although perhaps, with hindsight, he should have invested with a licensed broker rather

69

than with his brother. Nonetheless, the money would need to be replaced. The lease of William's grand house, Frognal Park, was sold (interestingly to another of my ancestors, John Francis Menet, as described in Chapter 21).

Despite the terrible tragedy of his brother's death and the loss of funds, work continued at a relentless pace for Robert and his career blossomed. In 1834, he was appointed City Solicitor. There were some perks to the job. The papers reported that on 27 February 1837 he and other dignitaries were entertained at the Mansion House by the Lord Mayor; Lord Melbourne was also present. The lifestyle was clearly taking its toll, however, and the *Sun* reported on 27 September 1839 that a petition had been received from Robert Finch Newman signed with his left hand and explaining that he was labouring under severe illness and had no hope of ever being able to resume his duties. The *Sussex Advertiser* of 30 September 1839 reported, 'Mr Newman, the City Solicitor, has resigned his situation being unable from overwork to continue the discharge of his duties. The *John Bull* reported on 27 October 1839 that the Court of Common Council had resolved to award him an allowance of £500 per annum for life. His wife, Dudley, was to receive £200 per annum for life. The decision was also made to split the two roles of City Solicitor and Comptroller of the Bridge Estates; it was finally recognised that this was too much for one person. Robert did not have long to enjoy his pension. He died on 28 November 1839, in Brighton and was buried there on 4 December. He was 47 years of age. He left his estate to Dudley.

One of Robert and Dudley's seven children was my great-grandfather, George Gunnell Newman, my paternal grandmother's father. He was born on 30 June 1827 at Artillery Place, Finsbury, and baptised on 24 July at St Luke's Church in Old Street. The 1841 census shows George and his two older brothers, Francis Browne Newman and Robert Rutland Newman at school, at an establishment run by a Mr Richard

Schofield at 21 Cannon Place, Brighton. According to an advertisement in the *Brighton Gazette:*

> Mr. Schofield receives a select number of pupils and prepares them for the public schools and the professions. The system of education comprehends a complete course of instruction in the Latin and Greek classics, with prose composition and versification. Young gentlemen are admitted when they can commence the Latin Accidence... the strictest attention is paid to the health, manners and morals of the young gentlemen, who are never left without superintendence. The premises have the advantage of a convenient playground. The education was also apparently conducted in large and airy school rooms.

Meanwhile George's widowed mother, sisters, and little brother (Ernest Peake Newman) were living nearby, in Russell Square, Brighton. At some point during the 1840s, the family moved back to north London for a time and then his mother settled in Eltham where she died in 1875, leaving an estate of around £4,000.

One of George's brothers, Robert Rutland Newman, became a solicitor and practised for a while from the family home which was at 14 Heathcote Street, Mecklenburgh Square in Bloomsbury. Another brother, Francis Browne Newman, trained as an architect and worked on Crystal Palace before taking holy orders. He became rector of Burton Latimer in Northamptonshire. George's youngest brother, Ernest, joined the 47th Regiment of Foot and he rose to the rank of Lieutenant-Colonel, serving in the Crimea, Malta, and Gibraltar. George also had three sisters who did not marry – Emily Gracilla, Charlotte Mary, and Dudley. Sadly, Dudley died in her twenties in Worthing; Emily and Charlotte lived on into their eighties, in the house, 'Queenscroft' on Eltham High Street, where they lived for many years with their mother.

At the age of thirty, George was a very eligible young man. He had, only a few months previously, been made a partner in the City of London law firm of Freshfields, which then became known as Freshfield and Newman. The *Atlas* of Saturday 30 May 1857 carried this report of a meeting of the Court of Directors of the Bank of England where a resolution was passed appointing Charles Freshfield and Henry Freshfield as joint solicitors to the Bank:

> The former gentleman, for the past seventeen years, has held this position with his late brother, Mr. James Freshfield. These two gentlemen have also addressed a circular to their clients in which they state that they have associated with themselves, as partners, William Dawes Freshfield, son of the late Mr. J. Freshfield, and Mr. G. G. Newman, a gentleman who has for some years past held a position of great trust in their offices.

1857 was also the year in which George married my great-grandmother Frances Josephine Dale (1837–1910). The *Gentlewoman's Magazine* carries a report of Frances Dale in 1857, then aged twenty, having married, at Eastbourne Church, to George Gunnell Newman, of Bank Buildings and Bexley. Her brother, Thomas Pelham Dale, officiated at the ceremony. George was about ten years older than Frances.

In the same year, George also took out a lease from the Vansittart family on Hurst Place in Bexley, 'a capital family residence', as the *Morning Post* described it. The house was only eleven miles from central London. The Newmans built stables and a coach house and, according to the Bexley Archives, were responsible for planting many beautiful trees, including a rare gingko. The main road, which used to pass in front of the house, was re-routed. George and Frances also added a schoolroom, where the windows were set high so that the children would not be distracted by the horses in the courtyard; children followed very soon after the marriage, beginning with Charles Frederick, who was baptised on 4 July 1858 at St Mary-the-Virgin, Bexley. Two more boys, Dudley and George Herbert, followed in very quick succession by three girls, Mary, Helen and Flora, with my grandmother, Kathleen Clara Newman, finally arriving in 1869. In a departure from family tradition, Kathleen was baptised at Holy Trinity Church in the parish of Lamorbey, Sidcup, a mile or so away from Hurst Place.

On 11th May 1868, Charles Frederick was admitted as a patient to the Normansfield Training Institution for Imbeciles, a private asylum for mentally handicapped of 'good social position'. There is no further mention of Charles in any of the family notices; his death from bronchitis at the age of thirty-seven in 1895 was not recorded in the newspapers. Records show, however, that his body was brought back from Normansfield for burial at St Mary-the-Virgin, Bexley.

Dr Down, who ran Normansfield, a brand-new institution, with his wife Mary had previously worked as physician at the Earlswood Institute for Mental Defectives. Down's Syndrome was named after him. He believed that children from upper-class homes often had a raw deal, as they tended to be hidden away in the servants' quarters. Charles was one of his first patients. Normansfield saw a rapid expansion, attracting pupils from all over the world. Dr. Down did not believe in the use of physical punishment and ran the institution along the lines of a large family home. There were pony rides and Punch and Judy shows for the inmates and they were also taught how to dress themselves and how to use money. The fees were, in the 1870s, £150 guineas per annum, which is more than a public-school education would have cost at the time. The other Newman boys, Dudley and George Herbert, were sent to a school in Hove and then to prestigious Charterhouse.

Business affairs would have occupied much of George's time after his marriage. Freshfields had some high-profile clients, including the Bank of England, the Eastern Steam Navigation Company, and the London, Chatham, and Dover Railway Company. George acted for John Scott Russell, the engineer, who was in partnership with Isambard Kingdom Brunel. In that capacity, he attended, in 1859, the inquest into the bodies of the stokers and firemen who lost their lives in the explosion off Hastings on board the SS Great Eastern, the largest ship ever built. The project had led to Scott Russell's bankruptcy some years before and probably contributed to Brunel's death.

The *London City Press* of 23 March 1861 reported that the prestigious gold and silversmith, Messrs Sarl of Cornhill, had displayed in its window a richly engraved tea and coffee service with a tea tray, and a handsome three-armed epergne and candelabra, destined for Mr George Gunnell Newman. It said, 'The railway company wished to acknowledge his ability, perseverance and energy in promoting the interests of the company, more especially in session of Parliament of 1860 and generally of their esteem and regard.' The railway company in question was the London, Chatham, and Dover Railway. Each line had to be authorised by a separate Act of Parliament and George was being rewarded for his role in steering the company through that process. The London, Chatham and Dover Railway's lines ran through London, northern and eastern Kent, to form a significant part of the Greater London commuter network. It was advertised in 1860 as offering, 'The shortest route to Canterbury by twenty-one miles.'

However, controversy was to follow. Parliament had established rules for railway companies to the effect that railway companies could only borrow one third of their authorised share capital, to ensure there was a correct balance between share capital and loans. Before any share capital could be taken, all the share capital had to have been subscribed for, at least 50% paid for, and payment proved to the satisfaction of a justice of the peace. The allegation was made that Freshfields – and it was George's name which was dragged through the papers – had come up with a scheme which circumvented these requirements. It all came to light with the bankruptcy of Sir Morton Peto, MP for Bristol, whose firm had been involved in building a line for the company between London Bridge and Victoria, with payment to be made in the company's shares and debentures. Peto had previously built the railway in the Crimea, used to transport goods and supplies, and had been knighted for his work. However, the allegation was that shares for the London Bridge to Victoria project were issued in the name of Peto and his associates and the railway accounts written up to make it look as if the associated cash payment had either been made directly to Peto and Co. or made to the railway company directly and lent back to Peto. No cash changed hands, but on the strength of these fictitious 'constructs', the statutory declarations were made before Justices of the Peace and authority was given to raise the loans. Once these transactions came to light, the financial markets stopped lending to the railway, and it became insolvent.

Peto named George as having given him this advice and as having drawn up the documentation. It appears as if Peto was determined to take George down with him. The *Kentish Chronicle* of 27 October 1866 reported him as questioning why more investigation had not been carried out by George:

> Anyone who knows anything of the affairs of the London, Chatham and Dover Railway must know that there was a man in connection with it, a man of unexampled energy, great talent and great force of character – a man whom nothing would stop, short of success. That man was Mr. George Newman, the partner of Mr. Freshfield. It was he who gave the board advice, from the very initiation of the undertaking until the breaking down of his health.

Charles Freshfield strenuously denied, on George's behalf, that their firm had done anything wrong, writing that they regarded any such attempts to borrow money as 'utterly indefensible'. Freshfields were replaced as solicitors to the company and the railway company was refinanced. It seems that George then took a break from practice. Charles Freshfield, meanwhile, had become involved in politics and was elected as the Conservative MP for Dover in 1865.

On 11 June 1870, a note appeared in the *London City Press* to the effect that Charles Freshfield would shortly be retiring from practice. The article also mentioned that George had joined the firm Dale and Stretton, which would henceforth be known as Newman, Dale, and Stretton. It reported, 'Mr. Newman is one of the younger sons of a late City solicitor, whose family have so long been identified with the Corporation.' The article also mentioned that George had been suffering from ill-health, due to overwork, but that he had been busy during his 'retirement' and that he had written a book, titled *The Summary of the Law of Bankers' Cheques*.

On 19 March 1872, a notice appeared in the *Morning Advertiser*, offering £50 to anyone who could help with information about several men, who had 'burglariously entered' Hurst Place on 29 February last and stolen silver cruet stands, electro-plated and silver forks and spoons and a small coffee service, all bearing a wheatsheaf crest. Gold, silver and copper Roman and early English coins and bronze medals of the opening of New London Bridge, the City of London school and the Queen's first visit to the City had also been stolen. The Reward would even be extended to an accomplice, if not to one of the actual felons. According to the *Woolwich Gazette*, the burglars also made off with around £5 in cash from the butler's pantry.

At his new firm, George soon found his way back to the forefront. According to the *Railway Times,* Volume 43 of 1885, his enterprising spirit and great powers of organisation resulted in him being selected to lead 'one of the boldest measures of private bill legislation promoted of late years – notably the project for the formation of an underground railway from Kilburn to the Marble Arch and from thence through the heart of London to Bow.

Frances became pregnant again, after a gap of many years and at the age of forty-one, on 1 April 1878 gave birth to a son, Rutland John Newman, at 22 Upper Wimpole Street, London. Sadly, Rutland never made it home to Hurst Place. He was baptised on 11 April at All Souls in Marylebone and died the same day. He was buried at St Mary's in Bexley on 17 April.

George died on 24 January 1885 at his London residence - 14 Ennismore Gardens, Kensington - and was buried on 28 January at St Mary's in Bexley. He was 57 years of age. The *Morning Post* of 4 February 1885 contained this brief obituary:

> Mr. George Gunnell Newman, of the firm Newman, Stretton and Hilliard, solicitors, of Cornhill, whose death has just been announced, was prominently associated with most of the important measures of parliamentary private bill legislation of the time. Mr. Newman served his articles with Freshfields and at an early age became a partner in that firm, a position he occupied for many years.

The will of George Gunnell Newman was sworn over £27,000. The *Illustrated London News* of 18 April 1885 went on to report that this sum was 'exclusive of various sums of money, amounting to upwards of £50,000, settled by him on his marriage and subsequently on his wife and children'. George's estate was left to Frances. The executors were Frances, her brother Cecil Marston Dale and George's brother, Frances Browne Newman. She moved out of Hurst Place in 1888 and an advertisement was placed in the *Kentish Mercury* on 2 March that year, for an auction of 'excellent furniture and effects'. This included oak furniture from the school room, a cottage piano by Collard and Collard, a massive chandelier and an ottoman, as well as a pony phaeton and 2400 choice plants.

Frances moved to Cold Blow, Bexley, to a house called St Mary Mount, with two of her daughters, my great-aunt Mary and my grandmother Kathleen. With the retinue of servants was the family's nanny, Susan Williams, who, according to the census, had been born in Glamorganshire in 1829.

By 1900, they were at Redhill House, Chislehurst, in the year in which Kathleen who was to marry my grandfather Francis Charrington. I have written about their lavish wedding in Chapter 4.

Kathleen came from a line of successful men and there seems no doubt that, when she married, she had hopes and dreams that her husband would be equally successful. Sadly, for this Dale descendant, better times were not to come. Later my father would write of her having a nervous breakdown after her husband lost most of his money in unlucky investments on the Stock Exchange. She carried disappointment with her to her grave and this certainly had an impact on my father and, indirectly, on me. This all makes more sense to me now through the further discoveries we have made about my ancestors and my insights from Jungian psychology.

CHAPTER 10: HONG KONG
My Life in a British Crown Colony

I did not know then that Hong Kong was the key to my future, although ever since I had seen the movie *Love is A Many Splendored Thing* in 1955, Hong Kong had held a fascination for me. In the film, taken from the novel by Han Suyin, William Holden plays the part of a married foreign correspondent who falls in love with a Eurasian doctor. I dreamed of going there one day and little did I know that the dream was not so far away. A perk of being a BOAC employee after the first year was flying anywhere in the world for ten percent of the fare. That is how I went on holiday to Hong Kong, only paying £36 for the flight. That holiday dramatically changed my life. As a result, I married a man I hardly knew and went to live on the other side of the world.

When I arrived as a bride in November 1962 (see Chapter 16 for how this came about), I was greeted at Kai Tak airport by a small group of Dick's friends and neighbours from Sha Tin, the duplex apartment in which I holidayed a few months earlier with my flat mates Sue and Laurie. We were the airline stewardesses to whom Dick had so kindly loaned his home through his neighbours, the three Australian Cathay Pacific pilots who lived next door, Bob Crockett, Brian Lewis and Peter Stockel. They were kindness itself in ferrying us around and showing us the sights of Hong Kong, as well as letting us into a few secrets about the private life of Dick Dennis. I was intrigued and could not wait to meet him. To us, Dick's home was heaven. There were Chinese servants to look after our every need, a wonderful view of the Sha Tin valley, and a swimming pool. We found the three dachshunds a bit of a nuisance with their constant yapping at every passer-by; little did I know that within a few months they would be my constant companions. Once married to Dick, I was mistress of the house.

My life in Hong Kong was idyllic looking back, but of course there were anxious times. For example, there were always refugees trying to escape from China across the border into what was then a British Crown Colony. There were challenges on a personal level too. I was homesick when I saw a BOAC bus collecting crew from the Miramar Hotel in Kowloon and my new husband was out all day. We were no longer on honeymoon and he was busy at work. Every morning, except Sunday, he drove down the windy road to park his car at the Kowloon post-office. From there he caught the Star Ferry to the central district of Victoria Island. A five-minute walk and he was at his office in Des Voeux Central, above the Dairy Farm supermarket. I had to find something to do that was familiar to me, so I started work as a volunteer at St Christopher's Orphanage, Taipo making use of my nursing skills. Dick knew about the home. He had met Bishop Hall who founded the orphanage in 1935. I was to go and see Miss Ethel Izzard, who oversaw the Babies' Section. The Reverend Herbert Osborne was the Superintendent from 1960 onwards; he and Miss Izzard had both been missionaries in China.

I drove out from our house one morning in November 1962, up the steep lane and turned right towards Taipo on the morning of my appointment with Miss Izzard. After about five miles along the Taipo road and through the village of Sha Tin, I came to the orphanage. It was a large rambling house with cottages surrounding it, overlooking the South China Sea. Miss Izzard came out to greet me and I felt at ease with her at once. She seemed pleased to have my offer of help. She led me into the babies' nursery and there they all were, mostly baby girls, with their bottles of milk propped up on a pillow. There were not enough staff to feed them, so I was at once allotted a baby to hold and feed. It took me back to my midwifery days in Belfast. It felt satisfying and helped me to remember the part of me that felt confident at knowing what I was doing. My new life was all so strange, and I had to find my own niche.

Our Hong Kong junk.

My new friend Barbara Brown, also recently married, in her case to an Australian Cathay flight engineer, Don, came to help. She was in tears; it was just before Christmas and the thought of the babies not having anyone to feed them upset her. I was more hardened, having been a nurse and witnessed human suffering at first hand from the age of 18. I found Miss Izzard delightful. She was unassuming and modest and had a whole history behind her of missionary work in China. I regret not having found out more, but my time there was short. I became pregnant and suffered from morning sickness, so, after only a month at the orphanage, I left. I told Miss Izzard, 'I can't believe it's happened so quickly,' to which she replied, 'Oh yes my dear, it can happen in a day.' I was to discover she came from Tunbridge Wells in Kent where Dick and I were to make our first home in England a few years later. I regret not having kept in touch. In a few months I had my own baby to feed: Richard Charles was born on August 30 at the Matilda Hospital up on the Peak on Hong Kong island. Dick had gone to another part of the New Territories to bring to our Chinese junk closer to home. Fortunately, Dick arrived home in time to drive me to hospital. It was also the week the Mandarin Hotel opened on the island.

Another long-lasting impact of my time in Hong Kong was that it was there my interest in astrology began. It started when Dick and I met Marcia and Whit Newton at a dinner party given by our neighbours, Roy and Paddy Davis. Roy was an 'Old China Hand' and he and his wife loved to entertain. He was also well-known for pony-trekking in Inner Mongolia in the 1920s and for introducing the Mongolian pony to Chinese horseracing. He knew Dick's father in Tientsin (now Tianjin) in the 1930s and had travelled with him and Dick's stepmother Virginia on the Trans-Siberian Railway from China to Moscow in 1938 when Dick was on his way to start boarding school in Sussex. The evening in 1965 is one I shall never forget, partly because Roy gave me information about Dick's stepmother (all explained in my book *All I Ever Wanted*), that Dick had apparently blocked from his memory, but also because this was the start of a friendship with the Newton family that was to be lifelong, including the holiday mentioned in the Introduction which I took with their daughter, Robin, in Northern California. The Newtons also lived in the New Territories in a Chinese village house, something very unusual at the time. Whit's family owned a boatyard, American Marine, and instead of paying a large rent for a European style house they chose to put money back into American Marine and economise. With Marcia's artistic talents the village house looked enchanting. I did not know about the rats running around at that stage of our friendship or how cold it was in winter.

Marcia opened-up a new way of thinking for me. As a vicar's daughter I had never ventured out of a conservative, Christian way of thinking about the world. Marcia's brother lived in San Francisco and made jewellery. He was unmarried, but he lived with a woman and they had a child together. I was shocked. I was also intrigued by Marcia. She was an artist, believed in astrology, and read palms.

It was incredibly sad when the day came for us to leave Hong Kong. Dick was insistent we kept to the plan he had articulated the night we met in August 1962 while dancing at the Blue Angel, Berkeley Street in London's West End, that once married with children he would return to England when it was time for them to start school. It was now 1969 and we were feeling less safe, especially because of the Cultural Revolution, which had begun in 1967 in mainland China. We were in the New Territories and we had the feeling that the Chinese could so easily come over the border at any moment. Many foreigners left at this time, particularly Americans. We were also mindful that Dick's father had lost everything in China in 1941 and felt it would be better to get out. We gave a farewell party for our servants. These included Ah Kong and Ah Choi, who had been our house servants, and Wah Po, who was our *fah wong* or general handyman and looked after our boat. Wah Po came with his wife. They did not wear shoes as they were boat people, but they seemed to enjoy the evening as much as anyone. We also invited Mr Mak of the Asia Company who had delivered our groceries daily from Kowloon, ten and a half miles away, including down our unmade road which could be treacherous during the rainy season. A Chinese restaurant provided the food which was magnificent.

We also had a farewell party to which we invited our friends, with food from the Peninsula Hotel in Kowloon including my favourite starter, crab meat and mango. The party was outside, in July, the middle of the typhoon season. We had almost finished dinner when the heavens opened. Dick was not at his calmest as our guests got up from their tables to help move things. Whit Newton, who worked for American Marine, took charge; he was used to far worse on a boat. Our guests were thankful to resume the party indoors, and we all danced to Herb Alpert and Chris Montez.

We kept in touch with Ah Kong and Ah Choi for many years, receiving letters and Christmas cards from them written by one of Ah Kong's daughters. When I accompanied Dick on business trips during the 1970s, we always met them and eventually we all travelled to Hong Kong as part of our Far Eastern holiday in 1978, nine years after we had left the colony. Ah Choi said, 'I will take my boys shopping.' They bought each of them a watch. My life in Hong Kong is so different from my life today, but I have always retained that sense of adventure which took me there and its influence upon me lives on.

CHAPTER II : THE DALES
Better Times to Follow

My remarkable great-great-grandfather Thomas Dale was born on 22 August 1797. We shall consider Thomas more in Chapter 13 but here we consider his family heritage. Records show that he was baptised at St James's Church in Pentonville on 17 September 1797 and his parents were William Dale and Mary Dale (née Smith). We know they also had three daughters, Mary, Elizabeth and Ann. Another daughter, Frances, died just a few weeks after her birth, in 1799. The family lived in Cumming Street, in what would have been a new house. The street was named after Alexander Cumming, a Scottish watchmaker and inventor who was, in 1775, the first to patent the design of the flush toilet but also, with his brother, involved in the development of Pentonville. Another famous resident of Cumming Street, before she met William Godwin, was Mary Wollstonecraft, author of *A Vindication of the Rights of Women*.

William Dale was born in about 1764 and his father's name was, apparently, Thomas. We do not know much about William's early life, apart from what can be gleaned from the writings of Helen Pelham Dale, one of his great-granddaughters. Apparently, William travelled to London in about 1780 and was descended from the Dales of Northumberland. Their family motto was *meliora sequor,* which my teenage grandsons, Tom and Hector, translated for me as 'better times to follow'.

William had an aunt, Peggy Dale, who corresponded with John Wesley. Peggy was born in 1744 in Bishopwearmouth, the daughter of Edward Dale. She and her sisters Mary, also known as Molly, and Anne came under the care of Margaret Lewen, thought to have been their aunt, when their father Edward Dale died in 1753. Margaret Lewen was described by John Wesley as a pattern to all young women of fortune in

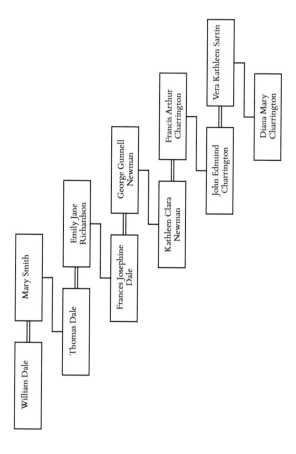

Descendant chart for William Dale.

England, a real Bible Christian. When they first met, as Wesley observed, she was 'about two and twenty and had about six hundred pounds a year in her own hands'. She gave Wesley a pair of horses and a chaise and, when she died, left him £1,000 in her will. She also left Mary Dale £1,000 and Anne and Peggy £100 each. Margaret's father, Thomas Lewen of Kibblesworth, survived her and threatened to challenge the will but seems to have decided against it because he received the residuary estate.

We know details of the correspondence between Peggy and John Wesley because seventeen letters from John Wesley to Peggy Dale (who, of course, met through Margaret Lewen) came into the possession of Canon Thomas Dale and were then passed to his son, Reverend Thomas Pelham Dale. Eventually they came into the possession of the Reverend Thomas Cyril Dale, another Dale descendant and a genealogist, who wrote a chapter called 'Durham Associations of John Wesley' in a book titled *Memorials of Old Durham*. Thomas Cyril states that he is not sure how the letters came into the possession of Canon Dale, presumably through his father, William. Helena Pelham Dale, William's great-granddaughter, in *The Life and Letters of Thomas Dale,* recounts that all that William left to the family was a portrait of himself and this packet of letters. The research Thomas Cyril Dale put together indicates that the male branch of the Dale line from whom Peggy Dale descends died out; she did have a brother, Edward Dale, born in 1752, but the male line is no longer extant.

John Wesley and Peggy began to correspond in 1765 and he wrote: 'How far do you find power over your thoughts? Does not your imagination sometimes wander?' Her address was The Orphan House, Portpatrick Road, Newcastle upon Tyne. This had been built by Wesley in the 1740s, but it was not used as an orphanage but rather as a centre for Methodist preaching. Peggy did marry – in March 1773 at St Andrew's Church,

Newcastle upon Tyne, to Edward Avison. However, he died in 1776 and she died in 1777, and they did not have children.

Peggy's sister, Mary Dale, also known as Molly, was another of Wesley's correspondents although his letters to her did not pass through the family. She married John Collison in 1769, again at St Andrew's in Newcastle, and they had several children, including George Dale Collinson, who was a barrister. They lived in Southwark. Peggy's other sister was Anne, who never married; she died in 1820 in Newcastle and left her money to the Collinson children but also to a Margaret and a Frances Dale. Probate was taken out in London

We may never solve the mystery of William's birth. What we do know is that he married Mary Smith at St Mary's Church in Islington, on 28 March 1790, a Sunday, with the curate, Thomas Walker, officiating. The witnesses were Henry Passmore, a neighbour, and Mary Smith, the latter presumably being the mother of the bride. The marriage was by licence, which William had obtained one year before. William was then residing in the parish of St Mary, Islington and Mary in the parish of St James, Clerkenwell.

William was a bookseller. He and Mary had their first daughter, Mary, in 1793 in Southwark and she was baptised at Christ Church. They moved to the parish of St James in Clerkenwell, and more children followed – Anne in 1795, Thomas in 1797, Frances in 1799 (she did not survive more than a few months) and Elizabeth on 7 December 1800. There is a record of Elizabeth having been baptised on 7 February 1801. Mary senior died in 1801 and there is a record of her burial at St James's Church, Clerkenwell on 31 May that year. William was then left with four small children, including my great-great-grandfather Thomas.

Helena Pelham Dale describes William as a scamp and a Bohemian. He was also described, many years later in his son's obituary, as being a man of some literary attainments. He remarried and went to the West Indies to set up a newspaper. He died shortly after that; with some reports stating that he 'succumbed to the climate'. No further details are known. Many years later, the Reverend Thomas Cyril Dale was making enquiries and found this in a publication known as *Caribbeana:*

> ...a certain William Dale went out to the West Indies in 1805 or 1800 to carry on a weekly newspaper. His second wife is supposed to have accompanied him and he is thought to have died shortly after his arrival. Reverend Dale enclosed the two wills of Adam and Robert Dale of Jamaica, of which the editor has made abstracts:

> Adam Dale, land surveyor, of the parish of Hanover. Will dated 30 September 1799. All real and personal estate to my friends James Symes of Saint Ann, Robert Stoney and Richard Evans of Trelawny for sixteen years for my reputed daughter, Elizabeth Dale, now an infant under one year, and if she die to Ann Morrison, Trustees to be Executors. Witnessed by Robert Ball, William Brown, John Barnby. Proved 23rd December 1799.

> Robert Dale of the parish of Hanover. Will dated 10 May 1804. My reputed daughter, Mary Mcallum Dale and my reputed son, Philip William Dale, £100 each. Nurse Sarah Hall, £100 and furniture. My nephew, John Dale, my heir at law, £150 if possible and recommend him to my respected friend and employer, George Brisset. The latter and John Foster to be executors. Witnessed by Agnes Robertson, Adam Gray, George Marvilier, proved 21st June 1804.

One wonders who Adam and Robert Dale were; presumably, they were relatives as otherwise what would have attracted William to go out there and how would their wills have been in the possession of Thomas Cyril Dale? George Brissett was a slave-owner in Montego Bay. One also wonders what sort of newspaper William was going to be involved in; most of the Jamaican newspapers at that time were run for the benefit of the slave owners and carried reports and offers for rewards regarding runaway slaves.

The records do not actually reveal the fate of William and his new wife. His children by Mary Smith were left with their mother-in-law. She was also asked to take in a relation by marriage – a young girl called Anna Dale - and was given money to do so. Thomas, according to Helena Pelham Dale, always regarded her as a sister.

The youngest daughter, Elizabeth Dale, never married. By 1841, she was living in a village near Kings Lynn – Grimston, Norfolk, with a farming family by the name of Lofty. There is no indication as to when (and why) she arrived in Grimston, described in *White's Gazetteer* as a populous and well-built village. Records show that the village was afflicted by Asiatic cholera in 1832 and that out of 60 cases, 26 died within a fortnight. Many villagers fled the location at that point. Elizabeth, assuming she was already living there, survived and eventually died there in 1870. She was buried on 22 October at St Botolph's, the local parish church. She did not leave a will, although many of the national papers mentioned her death in a brief notice.

There is a record of the death of Ann Dale of Bridge Street, Southwark in 1843 and of her burial in the vestry vault of St Bride's, Fleet Street on 16 February 1843. She was around 48 years old then and her cause of death was recorded as 'decline'. Was this Thomas's cousin or his sister? There was an Ann Dale living with the family when the census was taken in 1841, at 65 Lincoln's Inn Fields.

Thomas's other sister, Mary Dale, married William Mosyer at St Mary Cray in 1827. Helena Pelham Dale wrote that her father remembered William as being a Kentish squire, who farmed his own land and was the picture of what a yeoman farmer should be: stout, red-faced and cheerful, with a voluminous neckcloth, white breeches and a blue coat for Sundays. William and Mary did not have any children of their own. Mary died on 14 July 1869 at her home – Rose Croft in St Mary Cray – leaving a considerable estate. Probate was dealt with by one of Thomas Dale's sons, Lawford Torriano Dale, and by one of his sons-in-law, John Cunliffe Pickersgill-Cunliffe.

It is extraordinary to think that Thomas Dale was abandoned by his father not long after the death of his mother and became such a remarkable personality, as we shall see in detail in Chapter 13.

CHAPTER 12: MY MOTHER
A Vibrant Personality

When I moved to Hong Kong, my mother could no longer live her life through me with her unfulfilled longing to travel. After my wedding she took to her bed for a few weeks. My parents had never been abroad together. Our holidays as children were vicarage exchanges, or boarding houses in the Isle of Wight, or Minehead. On a few occasions we went on caravan holidays organised by Aunt Marjorie. My father did not join these. It is strange that he loved to talk about when he went to Naples and Monte Carlo in the 1920s and sad to think he never went abroad again. So, although it was hard for my mother when I married and took off for Hong Kong, she had the great excitement of travelling abroad for the first time to visit me there.

Dick paid for her to make her first visit to Hong Kong in 1963 for the christening of her first grandchild, our son Richard Charles Dennis. In retrospect, I wish Dick had paid for both of my parents to visit us for the very special occasion, although I wonder if my father would have been so far out of his comfort-zone that he would have found Hong Kong confusing. My mother's journey was extra-long, and she was delayed in Tehran. She enjoyed every minute of her stay with us, however, and she took to life in Hong Kong like a duck to water. My cousin Angela, my mother's niece, was staying with us for a year which was wonderful for them both. They could shop together while I was occupied with my young son. My mother adapted brilliantly, loved Ah Tim, our Chinese *amah,* went shopping in the Nathan Road, Kowloon, bargaining for bits of jewellery. She loved life in those days.

My mother had spent the first part of her married life as a curate's wife in Goodmayes and Brentwood, then a vicar's wife in Ilford and Walthamstow. All her friends were connect-

My mother Vera and her mother Florence.

ed to church and she led a very narrow life. My mother had a vibrant personality and loved company. Unfortunately, my father did not share these personality traits and would very often put a dampener on things. Meals always had to be on time for one thing and it was many years before I could bring myself to eat lunch after his regular time of 1 p.m. If the doorbell of the vicarage rang in the minutes leading up to 1 p.m. the caller would be greeted with a face like thunder. This was the same sort of face he wore at breakfast if the post only contained bills and no news of Cousin Geoffrey's death. It scared me. Later, I would occasionally see Dick make a similar face and that scared me too. How did my mother survive? I think because she was resilient, and the parishioners liked her. She had a sense of humour and made friends easily. She refused to let my father get her down. That is until he retired, and they moved to Pangbourne. At that point she was fifty-six and she must have felt despair at the realisation that she no longer had the role of the vicar's wife which was so central to her very being. The role she enjoyed so much and for which she had been groomed when she was sent away from the West Country at sixteen to become somebody different, ended abruptly.

93

So much was taken away from my mother when my father retired. She wrote to me consistently during the seven years we lived in Hong Kong. Every week the airmail arrived, and I would open it carefully for fear of tearing the thin paper. It was either addressed to Mrs Richard Dennis c/o Brutton and Co., Des Voeux Rd, Central Hong Kong, BCC (Dick's law firm) or to Francisville, 6 ¾ miles, Taipo Rd, Sha Tin, N.T., Hong Kong (our home until Dec '64 when we moved to Clifftop, 10 1/2 miles, Silver Strand, Clearwater Bay N.T., Hong Kong). Through Dick's generosity she visited us again in 1968.

My mother longed for us to return to UK. She had for some years used illness as a weapon, and my father and I used to tease her for being a hypochondriac. Looking back, I realise that was unkind of us. In the 1950s, tranquilizers and sedatives were prescribed at random with no thought of the outcome. I could see how down she was when we returned from Hong Kong in 1970. She had lost her enthusiasm for life. Only a year after my father's retirement, she had become dependent on pills. She had no relief from a much older husband who had no hobbies or interests outside his own little world. He could still command respect by being asked by the local clergy to take Sunday services, which he did right up until he died suddenly on Christmas Day, 1985. My mother by contrast had lost any sense of status or purpose.

Psychotherapy was not common when my mother first started to battle with depression. In fact, psychology and psychotherapy were not talked about in the world in which I grew up. I did not know the meaning of psychosomatic. Mental illness had a tremendous stigma and fear attached to it. People were sent away to lunatic asylums, and some had little hope of getting out. During my general nursing training in the 1950s I was attached to a psychiatric hospital for six weeks. It was St Luke's Woodside, Muswell Hill in North London, and it was an experience I shall not forget. Patients with schizophrenia were treated with deep insulin coma and some suffering from Obsessional Compulsive Disorder (OCD) were treated surgically with a leucotomy. These drastic measures are not used today, although Electro-Convulsive Therapy (ECT) was commonly used for depression until the 1970s.

I wonder how much my mother would have benefited from psychotherapy. On her first trip to Hong Kong, she made an insightful comment to me that I would later reflect upon a great deal. She asked, 'Whatever happened to your personality?' I had left life as a single girl in England, with a frustrated mother who wanted to live her life through me, for marriage with an older man. I was confused, living in a different world. Dick looked after me, but I lost my independence. He was the one who read the newspaper first; I had no opinions. How had I allowed to this to happen to me? I am thankful that I was put in touch with my unconscious through Jungian analysis. It helped me to recognise the 'wounded healer' within myself and thereby to cope with the vicissitudes of life. When I use the term 'wounded healer', I mean the scar left on me by seeing my mother, Vera, deteriorate. My determination not to slide as she did, became the driving force behind what I achieved after I returned from Hong Kong.

CHAPTER 13 : CANON THOMAS DALE
No Common Boy

Let us now turn to the remarkable Thomas Dale, my great-great-grandfather. He was the hook which enabled me to start writing my family history, as when I looked at the family tree my Uncle Harold had laboriously written by hand in 1966, I was daunted by the sight of hundreds of ancestors going back to the 1500s. Thomas was a clergyman, as was my father, so that seemed a good enough reason to focus on him, and besides, I have his portrait hanging in my sitting room. Also, I was aware of living in London and having easy access to the churches where he preached and carried out his parish work.

However, he turned out to be so much more than a parish clergyman. He was the first professor of English Language and Literature in England, a post he held at University College London, where my youngest son, James, Thomas's third-great-grandson, studied English in 1988. I have an admiration for anyone who achieves their goals in life, especially in adverse circumstances and Thomas Dale certainly did that. The more I researched Thomas, with the help of Debby and Steven, the more fascinated I became by him. What he achieved in his seventy-two years was remarkable indeed.

He survived a tough and emotionally deprived childhood, rather like Dick Dennis, the man I married. Both men lost their mothers at an early age but for different reasons. Thomas's mother died when he was four. By comparison, my husband was told his mother had died when he was three but did not learn the truth that she died much later until he was approaching sixty. I mention this as it is interesting how the early loss of maternal love appears to harden the character of a child. Both men, without parental support, achieved a great deal in their lives. Their own children were hugely important to them.

Thomas's grandmother, my fourth-great-grandmother, Mrs Smith, understandably had a low opinion of her son-in-law, William Dale, after he abandoned his children shortly after his first wife's death and travelled to the West Indies with a new wife. Mrs Smith managed with the help of supportive friends and relatives to gain a nomination for her grandson and a place at Christ's Hospital School in the City of London. This was established as a foundling hospital in 1552 and initially associated with freemen of the City of London. By the 18 century, it had stopped taking in foundlings and its remit had broadened to include others in need. Applicants could not be in receipt of parish relief although some were recommended by parish officers. Various accounts and obituaries suggest that Thomas was recommended by relatives – perhaps uncles – on his mother's side. Getting into the school was no mean feat; strict enquiries were made as to background and indeed one of Thomas's contemporaries was removed from the school because it was discovered that his place had been secured under false pretences. Christ's Hospital was also known as the Blue Coat School because of the distinctive blue uniform worn by the pupils, consisting of a blue frock coat and yellow stockings. Thomas' obituary in the *Cambridge Independent Press* states, 'It was within the walls of that institution that he received his early education, and seldom has a nomination to such a charity, obtained by private interest, been more thoroughly justified by its results.'

Thomas attended Christ's Hospital with William Trollope, who was the headmaster's son and who also went into the Church, later emigrating to Australia. He wrote a book titled *A History of the Royal Foundation of Christ's College* which was published in 1834, and he observed that the great mass of the children 'were destined for trade or some mercantile occupation and it was to equip them for the commercial life that the system of education at Christ's College was devised'. He explains how others, at the age of fifteen, found their way into the Deputy Grecians Form. From there, they could progress to the Grecians Form, which qualified them for the medical or legal professions, but some completed their education elsewhere. He then says that one such was Thomas Dale 'of Corpus Christi, Cambridge' whom he describes as 'my old schoolfellow and highly valued friend'.

There are, in fact, two versions of what happened to Thomas after he finished at Christ's Hospital School. According to the *Living Preachers' Portrait Gallery,* which came out in 1841, Thomas Dale then

> directed his attention to the business of a bookseller, but it was soon discovered that a secular employment was little adapted to the turn of his mind. The studious habits and the literary tastes he had acquired made his heart yearn after nobler things.

The article also states that Thomas became a sizar at Corpus Christi College, Cambridge, in 1818. A sizar was a student who funded his upkeep at university by performing menial tasks around the college; often a small grant would also be available from the college.

The second version comes from an 1854 obituary of Thomas's father-in-law, my third-great-grandfather, James Malcott Richardson. The Misses Barker of Greenwich were James's sisters-in-law (James having married Mary Barker in 1801). The obituary says James found a Latin usher for their preparatory school in Greenwich, in the shape of Thomas, described as a raw but intelligent youth from the Bluecoat School. The obituary, which was published in the *Sydney Morning Herald* on 28 September 1854, goes on to say that the boy, not liking his new duties, suddenly left without warning. It says further:

> Mr. Richardson, on receiving this information, immediately went in pursuit, inquiring in every quarter where there was a chance of hearing of the fugitive. Amongst the number was a wealthy relative of the youth, who, on learning the object of Mr. Richardson's visit, abruptly censured him for being about any

Canon Thomas Dale.

sort of trouble about so worthless a boy. Mr. Richardson's reply was characteristic. 'I see something about that boy which, by
God's providence, I wish to bring out. He is no common boy and
find him I will.' After many inquiries he did find him, took him
to his house, and after a severe lecture encouraged him to return
and become reconciled to his duties, with a promise that if he did
so, he would make a man of him. This promise, he faithfully per-
formed. The young man was enabled to go to university and keep
his terms, without relinquishing his situation.

The *Living Preacher* made enquiries of Corpus Christi and came up with the gem that Thomas 'was not distinguished for his application to Mathematics; he did not read for honours, but he was exceedingly diligent at applying himself to the study of general literature.' According to enquiries their correspondent made of the college, he was not a rowing man and kept little company.

Whilst at Cambridge, Thomas married James Malcott Richardson's daughter, Emily Jane Richardson, my great-great-grandmother, at St Michael's Church, Cornhill, in the City of London on 22 November 1819. Thomas is described in the church records as being 'of the parish of Greenwich'. Emily was sixteen years old and had been baptised in the same church in 1803. Because of her age, permission had to be sought from her father for the marriage. It was also while still at Cambridge that Thomas wrote the first of many books of poems – *The Widow of the City of Naïn*. It was published through his father-in-law's publishing company. The *Sun* of London reported its publication on 19 May 1820, describing it as an elegant and virtuous little volume.

Thomas and Emily's first son, Thomas Pelham Dale, was born on 3r April 1821 and baptised on 30 April 1821 at the church of St Alphege in Greenwich. His father's occupation was given as 'schoolmaster' and the family was living at Maze Hill. The next few years were busy for Thomas. He and Emily had many more children, details of whom are given in Chapters 17 and 19. Thomas received his bachelor's degree from Cambridge in 1822 and he was also ordained as a deacon in that year, followed by his priesting in 1823. His first Church appointment was as Curate of St Michael's Cornhill, where he and Emily had married.

From 1826, Thomas was Assistant Preacher at St Bride's in Fleet Street and then evening lecturer at the church of St Sepulchre-without-Newgate and morning preacher at the church of St Mary Abchurch. He was also taking in pupils at his home. The older Dale boys learned with their father's pupils, although Helena Pelham Dale writes that her father, Thomas Pelham Dale's, education there was 'desultory'. Then again, sciences were his first love, an interest he shared with his mother. They would often discuss 'the insoluble problem of perpetual motion'. She was probably less keen on his experiments on his little brothers and sisters, when he would give them electric shocks.

In 1828, Thomas was appointed Professor of English Language and Literature at University College, London, having initially applied for the Professorship of Roman Language and Literature (a position which went to his clerical colleague, John Williams). He stayed there for two years. It was not exactly a comfortable fit; Matthew Arnold described University College as that 'Godless institution on Gower Street'. Professor Arthur Burns's entry on Thomas in the *Oxford Dictionary of National Biography* describes how his lectures emphasised moral considerations in the appraisal of literature, and that, seeking to counteract the secularity of University College, he joined with John Williams and Dionysius Lardner in purchasing an episcopal chapel in Gower Street in 1828 and opening a 'theological institution' in 1829 with a divinity lectureship to which Dale was appointed. He became part of a movement to build a chapel at King's College and this he achieved, also becoming Professor of English Language and Literature there in 1836, a position he held for the next three years. At first, King's College did not award degrees and catered for young men aged between sixteen and eighteen, many of them preparing for entry to Oxford and Cambridge.

The first home the Dale children remembered was the Clock House in Beckenham, formerly occupied by Lady Annabel Byron, estranged wife of Byron. The children always thought the house was haunted. Helena Pelham Dale writes that her father remembered a square stone hall with a gallery round, and in the hall a heavy oak table, as well as a dark archway which terrified him. There was also a haunted hill, down which the children often raced at sunset, fancying they heard a hobbling step behind them. The ghost was supposed to be that of an old lady who had left directions in her will that she should be buried upright, ready for the day of judgment. Local superstition declared that she walked out at sunset. The Dale children also enjoyed the village fairs at Beckenham, where there would be plays depicting the Duke of Wellington and Napoleon Bonaparte. The showman would announce: 'There's the Dook a-leadin' of 'is men to victory, and there's Boney 'iding be'ind the trees for fear of the bullets.'

From the Clock House, Thomas would drive out with his manservant George on Sundays to the church where he was going to preach, as he was already in great demand as a preacher. When he took on the incumbency at St Matthew's, Denmark Hill, the family moved to Grove Lane in Camberwell, within walking distance of Herne Hill. Thomas ran a small school from the house, taking in fewer pupils as his church commitments increased. The priest and novelist Charles Kingsley (1819–1875) was also one of his students, as was the artist and philosopher John Ruskin (1819–1900). Thomas kept one of Ruskin's essays, which was on Lord Byron (1788–1824).

Ruskin described Thomas as his 'severest and chiefly antagonistic master'. According to the biography by Francis O'Gorman, Ruskin wrote to his father about himself and his fellow pupils that, 'Mr. Dale crams them and me beyond the bounds of our digestion.' However, surviving correspondence exhibits a surprising warmth and intimacy from Ruskin to Dale. The former frequently went to hear his old master preach, and Thomas's daughter, Frances Josephine Dale, my great-grandmother, had a poem by the great man dedicated to her, namely 'The King of the Golden River'.

Another pupil of Thomas Dale's was Edmond Oldfield, who subsequently worked with Ruskin on the east window of St Giles's Church, Camberwell and went on to become a curator at the British Museum and an expert on ecclesiastical restoration. Ruskin wrote in his unfinished autobiography

Praeterita (written1885–1889) that there were also boarders – the sons of Colonel Matson at Woolwich and of Alderman Key of Denmark Hill, and Willoughby Jones, who went on to become a Conservative politician and MP for Cheltenham. Thomas also taught Alexander Penrose Forbes, son of Lord Medwyn, a Scottish judge, who went on to be made bishop of Brechin, becoming the first member of the Oxford Movement to be ordained to the episcopate. Often referred to as the 'Scottish Pusey,' Alexander Forbes is quoted by Helena Pelham Dale as having very fond memories of his time at Beckenham, being taught by Thomas and of the wise advice given to him by Emily. Pupils also recalled Emily reciting the Waverley novels of Walter Scott by heart, an indication that she was also a person of academic ability.

In 1835, Thomas was appointed as Vicar of St Bride's in the City of London. With this living came a new house, at 65 Lincoln's Inn Fields, a house with four storeys and a basement, with crinoline-shaped balustrades to the main stone staircase. One can picture the young Dales, racing up and down the stairs, excitedly exploring their new home, although they would have had to be quiet as Thomas often held tutorials, as part of his King's College work, upstairs.

For a description of Thomas (and his family's) time at St Bride's, we can turn to the *History of St Bride's – The Great Fire to 1944* by Walter H. Godfrey:

> Dr Thomas Dale, a man of note, ... became Dean of Rochester. He had first come to St Bride's in 1826, and was instituted to the vicarage in 1835, aided by the support of Sir Robert Peel. His portrait, by John Lewis, used to hang in the vestry room and an aquatint engraving of it exists. He was a most attractive preacher; his eloquence and learning filled the Church.

Mrs Carr, a resident in the parish for twenty-five years and in turn scholar, teacher and superintendent of the parish school, in writing her recollections of this period, tells how on Sundays it was often impossible to secure a seat in the church. She recounts the imposing spectacle of Dr Dale's entry and passage up the centre aisle, followed by his wife and twelve children, whilst immediately behind him came the wealthiest parishioner, a glass merchant, also followed by twelve children of his own.

This was a peak period, whilst the parish was still residential, and so great was the demand on the church that an additional building was erected, Holy Trinity in Gough Square, on a site given by the Goldsmiths' Company. The foundation stone was laid on 3 October 1837, but the new church did not last 100 years. The coming exodus of the residential population of the City was not foreseen, but once it started it was continuous and Holy Trinity was pulled down in 1913.

John Alonzo Clark, in *Glimpses of the Old World,* which was published in 1840, writes of having turned up one Sunday morning, hoping to hear Dr Dale, but he was preaching at St Sepulchre's and so the service was taken by Reverend Kelly instead. Mr Clark found the curate's style to be too florid and artificial. He also commented that the church was meant to take two thousand and was always full when people were expecting Dr Dale:

> It was certainly well-filled the morning I attended. Not only was every seat and aisle filled, but every standing place within the walls of the church was literally wedged in with an unbroken mass of human beings.

The novelist George Eliot (1819–1888), on a visit to London with her brother Isaac, heard Thomas preach at St Bride's one Sunday morning in 1838. She was an admirer of his poetry. She found his sermon interesting. She was less impressed with the lack of reverence she found at St Paul's during Evensong later that day.

Thomas's star was rising. However, with such a large family and no independent means, extra money was always welcome. *The Times* reported on 21 December 1840 regarding 'The Golden Lectureship in the Gift of the Haberdashers' Company'. The Company was looking for a new lecturer, who would keep together 'the most remarkable weekday congregation that exists in the City of London'. There was, in *The Times'* view, only one man for the job. In less than six years at St Bride's, Thomas had raised the money to build the new church at Gough Square, raised the money for two new schools and opened a Provident Society, a lending library, and a lecture room. All this did not come at the expense of his preaching – Thomas was also preparing three, and often four 'first rate discourses each week'. The report went on to ask,

> And what has been his recompense in worldly things? Never, in any one year, has the income of his benefice sufficed to maintain his household. Never has his preferment yielded anything approaching the income of a leading clerk in one of the Fleet Street banking houses.

A report appeared in the *Worcester Journal* of 26 October the same year to the effect that the Prime Minister, Sir Robert Peel (1788–1850), had presented a vacant canonry at St Paul's to Reverend Thomas Dale, Vicar of St Bride's. The intimation was, apparently, presented to Reverend Dale in a very handsome letter from the Premier himself, commending him for his exemplary efforts at St Bride's over the previous eight years. The report also noted that the Canonry had yielded to its previous incumbent an annual income of £2,300. Under the Church Reform Acts, its revenue had been reduced to £1,000 per annum, but with it came a fine old house in Amen Court. Helena Pelham Dale quotes Peel's letter to Thomas in full:

> Sir – When in power, in 1835, I appointed you the minister of an important and populous district of the Metropolis, in the confident expectation that your appointment would promote the spiritual welfare of that district.

> My expectation in this regard has been fully justified, and I have had the satisfaction of receiving ample testimony to the zeal and ability with which you have discharged the duties of a Parish minister.

For the purpose of rewarding your successful exertions and of encouraging others in the faithful discharge of their several functions, I have recommended to her Majesty that you should be selected for the vacant Canonry of St Paul's and her Majesty has been graciously pleased to approve of my Recommendation. I am Sir, your faithful Servant. ROBERT PEEL.

Helena Pelham Dale also writes that, as his fame grew, all Thomas's affection was bestowed on his mother's side of the family. News of his rise in the Church reached his 'kinsmen in the North' and they wrote to him. It was at that point that Thomas began to use the family crest. The *Evening Mail* of Wednesday 20 November 1844 contains this testimonial to Thomas which describes the crest:

A few of the friends and admirers of the Reverend T. Dale, residing in the parish of St Sepulchre, of which church the reverend gentleman has been evening lecturer for sixteen years, have determined to present him with a piece of plate, 'in testimony of their high estimation of his ministerial services' and of his unfailing eloquence in the cause of charity.'

We have had the opportunity afforded to us by Mr. Turner of Ludgate Hill, the manufacturer, of seeing this very handsome and chaste testimonial. It consists of an elegant epergne with three branches, springing from a massive pedestal and ornamented with leaf foliage. Its weight is about 100 ounces. Beneath the branches, at the foot of the pedestal, the arms of the reverend gentleman, a pelican with the motto 'Meliora sequor,' are handsomely engraved on a shield. The following inscription is engraved on the upper part of the pedestal:

Presented to the Reverend Thomas Dale MA, Canon Residentiary of St Paul's and Vicar of St Bride's by a few friends from St Sepulchre as a token of their high estimation of his ministerial services as evening lecturer during the space of sixteen years and of his great and successful exertions in promoting the interests of the various charities of the parish – 1844.

The testimonial must be as gratifying to the reverend gentleman as it is deserved.

The epergne was left on Thomas's death to his eldest son, Thomas Pelham Dale, who in turn left it to one of his sons, Herbert Dixon Dale, vicar of Hythe, 'along with a clock which used to belong to the Bishop of London'.

In July 1846, Thomas was appointed as Vicar at St Pancras's, perhaps appropriately the patron saint of children. To say that he had his work cut out with this new parish is perhaps an understatement. One hundred years before, the parish had been classed as 'rural', with perhaps a thousand residents. When the 1841 census was taken, there were 128,479 souls recorded as living in the parish – and this had increased in the six years between then and Thomas's incumbency to upwards of 140,000. It covered an area of 2600 acres. The living was, according to the *Evening Chronicle* of 10 July 1846, worth £1,500 per annum. The living for his predecessor, Reverend James Moore, who had died, was £2,000 per annum but it was reduced; the consensus seemed to have been that this vast parish had been too much for Reverend Moore and there was already talk of dividing it up into more manageable parishes. To Thomas, his new stipend must have still seemed a considerable step up; his income at St Bride's had been £500 per annum. He kept his lectureship at St Margaret's, Lothbury although there were 'rumblings' in the papers from anonymous correspondents that he ought now to vacate it, to make room for a more impecunious churchman.

On the Feast of the Epiphany two years ago, I decided I would go to St Pancras New Church opposite Euston station to attend the 10am Eucharist. I set off on the ten-minute walk from my home in Mayfair to Oxford Circus, and on to the Victoria line to Euston, just two stops. A short walk and I arrived at the church, a quarter of an hour before the service was due to begin. The lady taking the service was standing in for the vicar who was on holiday, but I had the good fortune to meet the historian for the church, who seemed very pleased to meet me, and told me Canon Dale had done a huge amount in putting St Pancras's on the map after its consecration by the Bishop of London in 1822. He was only its third vicar.

While Thomas Dale was being considered for St Pancras's, his name was also 'in the hat' for the proposed new Bishopric of Manchester, according to the *Bristol Times and Mirror* of 26 September 1846. The other candidate was Reverend Henry Montagu Villiers, vicar of Bloomsbury, who did eventually become Bishop of Carlisle and then Bishop of Durham, a few years later. In an article that appeared in the *Illustrated London News,* much later in Thomas' career, the suggestion was made that Sir Robert Peel would like to have seen Thomas become a bishop. However, Sir Robert Peel had resigned that summer, over the Corn Laws.

Thomas made an address to the parishioners in 1847, in which he mentioned that in parts of the parish, there were hundreds of children without a school, thousands of adults without a church, and where, in consequence, the moral condition of the people 'is such as would be a reproach not only to a Christian but even to a civilised country.' He also mentioned the fact that in that year alone, there had been 140 illegitimate births in the local workhouse, a testament to the prevalent moral depravity. He made considerable efforts to reform the parish. The *Lincolnshire Chronicle* reported on 17 November 1848 that the Queen Dowager, Adelaide (the widow of William IV), had sent him £200 for the building of no fewer than ten new churches. The *Illustrated London* News reported on 19 October 1850 the consecration of Holy Trinity Church, Haverstock Hill, 'The third of the twenty new district churches which the Reverend Dale hopes to see erected in his present overgrown parish.' He also responded to the demand of more parish seating by restoring St Pancras's Old Church. He had the exterior re-faced and a new tower built. In the mid-1860s, a few years after my great-great-grandfather's incumbency, the novelist Thomas Hardy (1840–1928) was an apprentice architect in the parish and oversaw the excavation of part of the churchyard during the construction of the Midland Railway London Terminus. He returned to Dorset in 1870 due to health, but the tree around which he re-arranged headstones is a wonderful feature of the churchyard today. I was delighted to visit one day and see both the restored church and the famous tree.

Thomas had, as mentioned, inherited a difficult parish and he would face even more of an uphill struggle without Emily at his side when she died in 1849. Helena Pelham Dale describes Thomas's grief at her loss as being 'as deep as it was inexpressible', an interesting turn of phrase. Work in the parish was relentless. The idea had already been mooted that new churches were needed; as Thomas observed, it was impossible for him to get to know his flock when they were so numerous. His ideas were met with some resistance from certain quarters as they were going to cost money. The 'Vestry' was opposed to any scheme that might fetter its discretion in setting church rates or indeed in levying them at all. Certain accusations were even made that Thomas was somehow trying to turn the situation to his own financial advantage. The *Lloyd's London Weekly Newspaper* seemed to 'have it in for him', referring on 7 July 1850, to the fact that he had given his younger son, Lawford, a curacy within the parish and presented older son, Thomas Pelham, with the rectorship at St Vedast's Church: 'A pleasant start in life for a young clergyman.'

Something my great-great-grandfather had to consider was the lack of burial space, in such a populous district. In 1853, he laid the foundation stone of the first extra-mural cemetery for the metropolis, at East Finchley. This was much needed. In 1850, Dr John Simon had described, in his report to the Commissioners of Sewers, how densely packed the burial grounds within the metropolitan area were and how the vaults beneath the churches were 'in many instances overloaded with materials of putrefaction and the atmosphere which should have been kept pure and without admixture for the living was hourly tainted with the fœtid emanations of the dead.' By this time, Emily had been buried in a private vault at St Pancras New Church and Thomas's sister Anne Dale and two of their children had been placed in the vestry vault at St Bride's. This must have played on Thomas's mind as discussions on burial space took place in Parliament and in the Press.

In his New Year's address on 31 December 1858, Thomas told his flock that he was beginning to think the time had come for him to resign from his post as incumbent of St Pancras, saying that he felt himself daily more and more unequal to his sphere of duty. Montague Villiers, who had by then become Bishop of Carlisle, read of Thomas's plans in *The Times* and wrote to express sympathy, and asking him to reconsider, saying he wished he were nearer to cheer him. 'You know it is not a post I coveted, but still you have done such great things. The Lord has made you so useful in the midst of a Godless Vestry – in the face of opposition where support ought to have been looked for.'

Not long after, the *London Daily News* of 22 June 1860 reported:

> At the vicarage 1 Gordon St, Gordon square, a presentation was made to TD by the congregation of a candelabra worth £200 and cash of £400. He gave a speech at considerable length during which he mentioned the chance had come up of a country living in 1853 but he decided to stay at St Pancras to achieve what he had set out to achieve, namely to reduce the parish to manageable districts.

Later in 1860, Thomas was appointed Rector of Therfield, near Royston in Hertfordshire. The rectory, according to Helena Pelham Dale, was a handsome, old-fashioned house, the kitchen built into part of an old monastery wall. The population was poor and agricultural, their main occupation being turkey breeding. Helena goes on to say that at one time, the villagers suffered greatly from fever, caused by bad water. They drank and cooked with water from a green and stagnant pond. Thomas sank a well at his own expense and put a pump in it. The Rectory also had a coach-house attached; the *Hertford Reform and Mercury* of 3 October 1863 reported that one Bernard Preston was tried and sentenced for breaking into the coach house and stealing a pair of shoes from William Gatward, Reverend Canon Dale's coachman. With him as curate was the Reverend Henry John Desborough, one of the sons of Thomas's old friends from his Camberwell days.

By 1861, the house at Amen Court was occupied by Thomas' younger children along with Mary Raven, one of Emily's nieces. Also, in residence were the Verger of St Paul's, James Christopher Laban, and his wife. James Laban was a former publican and foreman for a silk manufacturer. Thomas himself, when the 1861 census was taken, was living in Therfield with his unmarried daughter, Rose Ann Murray Dale, a friend of hers, a maid, and a butler.

From nearby Therfield Heath, Thomas could have seen the cathedral at Ely and King's College, Cambridge. In 1869, William Gladstone wrote to him, to offer him the Deanery of Ely, but Thomas turned it down on grounds of ill health. However, he accepted Gladstone's next offer and was appointed Dean of Rochester in April 1870. His predecessor, Robert Stevens, had been there for almost fifty years. Only three weeks into his post, and at the age of 72, Thomas died suddenly on 14 May. He was buried at Highgate Cemetery, and from his grave could be seen many of the churches he had caused to be built. His daughter, Rose Ann Murray Dale, was laid to rest beside him in 1890.

I spent several hours in the British Library one weekend and a very rainy day with Steven Saxby learning more about Thomas Dale. Steven, who was completing a PhD on the closure of churches, made a list of places we should visit, connected to Thomas and his son Thomas Pelham Dale. It was a memorable day, and the rain did not take away from our enjoyment. Steven took a video of me explaining the significance of each place we visited. The medieval parish church of St Michael, Cornhill, was our first port of call. The medieval structure was lost in the Great Fire of London 1666 and replaced by the present building traditionally attributed to Sir Christopher Wren. This is where Thomas was curate and married Emily Richardson in 1826. Unfortunately, the church was not open. After many other churches and a look at two drawings of Thomas in the library of the National Portrait Gallery, we visited King's College Chapel where Canon Thomas had been a lecturer, and, finally, Amen Court where Thomas died at the home of his son Thomas Pelham.

I found knowing about my connection to Thomas and the churches where he preached in London helped me settle down to my new life after Dick died in 2007. I felt connected, rooted. As a vicar's family we had moved around a lot and I did not feel as if I belonged anywhere. In fact, if I told people I was born in Essex, I was teased. 'Essex girl,' they said, pejoratively. Now, I can revel in my pride that so many churches and other places in central London, not far from where I live, are associated with my great-great-grandfather, the remarkable Thomas Dale.

CHAPTER 14: BACK IN ENGLAND
Life at Island Farm

We had bought a house in Kent called Black Barn in Wittersham, which we had used when back on leave in the UK in 1964, 1966 and 1968. After a few months at Black Barn, we knew it would prove too small for it to be our permanent home, so Dick and I found Island Farm in Biddenden. It was within our budget of £20,000 and it was to be where we lived for the next thirty-four years. It was a sixteenth-century half-timbered merchant's house, from the time of the weaving industry in the Weald of Kent. We fell in love with it as soon as we walked through the front door and straight into the large oak-beamed drawing room. The ceilings were high which would have accommodated the looms at the height of the weaving industry. From there a door led into the hall, a windowless room, with an oak beam from floor to ceiling in the middle. This had been the kitchen until the previous owners had added on something more modern three years before.

We learned from our French neighbour, Paulette Hotchkiss, that a Mrs Stretton had lived at Island Farm for many years and her kitchen had been the windowless room, now the hall. She used to be out in the rose garden at 5 a.m. tending the roses, which were magnificent, many of them of an ancient variety. A few years later, I went to visit the psychic and astrologer Russell Grant in London and he told me he saw an old lady in a rose garden. Dick was completely unperturbed when he heard this, 'Oh yes, I often feel her beside me in the garden.' So, we had a haunted garden, and later our son Richard sensed a presence in the far-attic bedroom. He refused to sleep there. Many years later, Lisa, his wife, felt the same, and so we accommodated them instead in the room above the newly built double garages at the end of the short drive. Our garden at Island Farm was Dick's pride and joy and it was open at least twice a year to the public, in aid of the Red Cross and the Tenterden Day Centre. One year it was ruined by a storm and it was a sad day indeed: I think we had three only visitors.

We had many exciting times at Island Farm which I describe more in Chapter 18, but there was another side to my life in Kent. I was coming up for forty, had a husband who was embarking on a new career, and three sons who were at school all day, in fact two of them at boarding school. I needed something to do. That is why I set up the Kent Astrological Society. We used to invite various speakers to our monthly meetings, mostly people I met at meetings of the Astrological Association of Great Britain.

It was through one of these, Liz Greene, that I was introduced to the ideas of Carl Jung. Liz was a very gifted woman, originally from California, and training to be a Jungian psychologist. Liz said, as we were sitting by the pool in our garden, 'Diana, you are bored. You should go into Jungian analysis.' She recommended I learn from Hella Adler, wife of the well-known psychologist Dr Gerhard Adler, and I began meeting her twice a week. Although Dick paid for my analysis and training, I think he resented my analyst as he always delayed paying her fees. Perhaps it made him feel unsafe. This was unknown territory to him, over which he had no control. The purpose of a Jungian analysis is 'individuation', leading to achievement in reaching your potential. Outside events are understood with the help of a skilled analyst, sometimes with the use of dreams. Sometimes the unconscious, by way of dreams, reminds us that what we are thinking consciously is keeping us on the wrong path. For my own part, I felt compelled towards individuation, to reach my potential.

'Synchronicity' is another Jungian concept, which holds that events are 'meaningful coincidences' if they occur with no causal relationship yet seem to be related. I had a chance conversation with the mother of one of the boys' friends, while shopping in Tenterden. She told me she was doing A-levels

The family gathered at Island Farm.

in English and the History of Art. Then there was a push for me to study A-levels from someone I met at a party. When Hella Adler suggested the same, I knew it was time for me to become a mature student.

A-levels changed my life as they started me on a journey to rediscover myself. That said, I was out of my comfort zone as I entered the basement room in Queensgate Terrace, Kensington with four young people who had all failed and were re-sitting their A-levels. I did not understand a word of *Othello,* the Shakespeare play on our syllabus, and T.S. Eliot was a mystery to me. Our teacher, Jill Brown, was very strict and we had to hand in three essays a week. I told her on one occasion that it would not be possible for me to write all three that week as I had to accompany my husband to the Dorchester Hotel for a Cable Television lunch. This was in 1980. The guest of honour was the former Prime Minister, Harold Wilson. Mrs Brown would not accept this as an excuse and told me she wanted my essay in on time. I was coming to the end of the A-level course and passed one of my son's friends in the corridor of the college. He asked me if I had filed in my UCCA form yet. I did not know what he meant, but soon found out that was the application form for university. Of course, I wanted to go to university. It was unthinkable to stop with English now. I was loving it. Rather than give up on life, as my mother sadly did, I was reaching my potential. I was finding a way.

CHAPTER 15: JAMES MALCOTT RICHARDSON

Bookseller and Philanthropist

James Malcott Richardson (1771–1854), my third-great-grand-father, was the father-in-law of Canon Thomas Dale and, of course, the father of Thomas's wife Emily. He married three times. His second wife was my third-great-grandmother Mary Barker and her mother, Mary Murray, was said to be one of the Murrays of Blair Atholl. Thomas Cyril Dale tells us that Mary Barker and her sister Jane recollect an aunt of their mother's, 'old Aunt Murray' declaiming in broad Scots: 'Eh, my dears, we come of a grand hoose.'

Emily had an older brother, Lawford, born in 1802 and an older half-sister, Sophia, born in 1799 by her father's first marriage to Sophia Hart, but many more followed: Pelham (b.1804), Malcott (b.1806), Sabrina (b.1807) Helen (b.1808), Magdeline de Visme (b.1810), Murray (b.1811), Clara Arundel (b.1812), Arundel (b.1814), Frances Mary (b.1815), Pennington (b.1816) and Guildford Barker (b.1817). Malcott died aged four in 1810, Sabrina aged ten months in 1808 and Arundel aged eighteen months in 1815. All three were buried at St Michael's, Cornhill, in the New Vault.

The Richardson children grew up at 23 Cornhill, opposite the Royal Exchange. James Malcott had gone into partner-ship with his Uncle, William Richardson, and a cousin, John Richardson, in 1797, as a printer and stationer. William, who had come to London from Headingley in Yorkshire, had two shops – one underneath the Royal Exchange and one opposite. William did not have sons to inherit the business and when he died, in 1811, John inherited the shop underneath the Royal Exchange and James Malcott the shop opposite. James Malcott became a very wealthy man, through a connection he estab-lished with the East India Company.

On 27 April 1817, only a fortnight or so after the birth of her last child, Mary died. The *Morning Post* reported that she left 'eleven children to lament the loss of a most inestimable mother.' She was thirty-six years of age. James Malcott re-married, on 31 July 1819, to one Jane Barker, his sister-in-law, at St Lawrence's Church, Ramsgate. They did not have any children. This was what was known as an 'illicit marriage' under the Table of Kindred and Affinity in the *Book of Common Prayer*. At the time the marriage took place, however, it was not specifically forbidden by law, but it could be voided by any interested party. The Marriage Act of 1835 introduced an absolute prohibition on such marriages but introduced validation for those – such as James Malcott and Jane's – which had already taken place. Perhaps that is why they were married in Ramsgate, away from prying eyes. Emily was a witness at the wedding, along with Thomas Dale, then a young curate. Perhaps his father-in-law's marriage, played upon Thomas' mind; he campaigned vigorously for the repeal of the 1835 law in the months before Emily died, writing, 'I cannot see the expediency of a law which is observed only by the scrupulous, evaded by the wealthy and defied or disregarded by the poor.' Emily married Thomas in November 1819 – at the age of sixteen – only a few months after her father married her aunt.

John Malcott's son Lawford was a member of the Stock Exchange and lived with his family in Eltham; Thomas Pelham Dale remembered going to visit them. Emily's older half-sister, Sophia Anne, married John Bryan Courthope and died in childbirth in 1833, leaving a daughter, Sophia Helen, who was brought up by Emily's father, her own father having died only a few years after her mother.

This was, as can be seen from James Malcott 's obituary, mentioned earlier, a recurring theme – his family home was something of a sanctuary, not just for members of the immediate or indeed wider family, but also for 'waifs and strays', children whose parents were on service with the East India

Descendant chart for William Malcott.

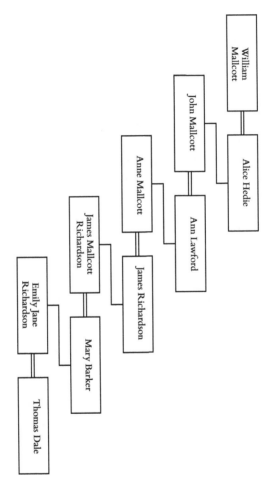

Company, for which he was an agent, and for orphans such as Thomas. The household in which Emily grew up – 23 Cornhill – was a busy one, with baby after baby arriving, until her mother died, a matter of a fortnight after the birth of the youngest, Guildford Barker. Emily was then just fourteen years of age; no doubt much of the responsibility for the younger children would have fallen on her.

James Malcott was born around 1771 in London and his father was a coal merchant in the area around Old Street. The Richardsons, according to Thomas Cyril Dale, came from the Leeds area. James's youngest son, Guildford Barker, took up the coat of arms of the Richardson family from North Bierley in 1863, and James Malcott's uncle, William, was said by his descendants to have used a seal bearing those arms. The seal was, in the 1920s when Thomas Cyril Dale published his findings, in the possession of one of William's great-great grandsons, Professor Francis Gibson Baily, electrical engineer.

However, Thomas Cyril Dale was only able to trace the family line 'reliably' back to a Robert Richardson, born in about 1660, a clothier from Great Woodhouse. Clothiers produced broadcloth from wool and Great Woodhouse was just outside Leeds. Records show that Robert married Sara Gammel in 1786 by licence; he is said to have been 'of the parish of Great Woodhouse'. Robert died in 1704 and was buried at St Peter's in Leeds. One of Robert and Sarah's children was John Richardson, baptised in 1691 and married in York in 1722 to twenty-year-old Mary Wilkinson, who was from Leeds. Mary and John had several children, including James Malcott's father James Richardson, who was born in 1737. Other than the fact that he was a coal merchant of Old Street, there is very little information on him.

James Malcott's mother, my fourth-great-grandmother Anne Malcott, was the daughter of John Malcott, a stone mason, who died in 1766 and is commemorated on a plaque in the ruins of Greyfriars church, near St Paul's, as 'citizen and mason of London'. John's business was based in Newgate and two generations of Malcott followed him as stone masons; the youngest worked with Thomas Cubitt on many buildings of note. John Malcott's uncle, also named John, was groom to the third Earl of Carlisle and left the family a lot of money and silver when he died in 1741, although his epitaph in the chancel of the church at Bulmer in Yorkshire reads:

> For all my Pains and Troubles from my Birth
> All that I've gained is but my Length of Earth.

It was from the Malcott side that James undoubtedly derived considerable wealth; the family owned many properties in London and in Martlesham in Suffolk under trust and lease, to which James Malcott alluded in his will. He himself inherited a lot of silver and houses in Marylebone and in Air Street, Westminster from his grandmother, Ann Malcott, *née* Lawford, who died in East Greenwich in 1790. As an aside, the Malcotts and the Richardsons seem, many years later, to have 'fallen out'; there was a case in Chancery in 1873 – Richardson v. Malcott, in which Emily's youngest brother, Guildford Barker, who had taken up the Richardson family coat of arms, was the plaintiff.

James Malcott as a young man was given a helping hand; he was apprenticed to his uncle, William Richardson, born in 1734 in Headingley, who was a stationer and bookseller with premises in Cornhill and under the Royal Exchange. William had become a very wealthy man and took on another nephew, another John Richardson, as an apprentice. William was married but only had one daughter, Ann, who married a surgeon, John Baily (brother of a famous astronomer, Frances Baily). Ann was, at the time of her marriage, esteemed to be 'one of the handsomest women in the City.' William left the business to his nephews, James Malcott and John James Malcott. James carried on with the business at Cornhill while John took on the business at the Royal Exchange. It is a little confusing that James Malcott Richardson also had a brother named

John Richardson, who became a mercer in Piccadilly but died in Paris in August 1814, on his way back from a silk-buying expedition to Lyons. This John Richardson is buried in Père Lachaise.

James Malcott made a lot of money himself, as a stationer and bookseller. One of his shrewdest moves was to buy the copyright from Captain Marryat (of Children of the New Forest fame) of *The Code of Signals for the Maritime Service,* which came out in 1817 and sold very well in many countries. This copyright is also alluded to in his will, of which Thomas was one of the executors, along with Emily's brothers. It is interesting that Thomas Dale also kept up the link with the East India Company; he was one of the examiners for the East India College (also known as Haileybury College). Perhaps Thomas did this in gratitude for the man who showed so much faith in him when he was a boy and would later become not only his patron but his father-in-law.

CHAPTER 16: DICK DENNIS
The Catch of Hong Kong

I like to recall the night I met Dick Dennis. It was 15 August 1962. I need to be reminded of how he used to be - lively and decisive. He was a fun person - generous and humorous - and later, devoted to his family. He died of vascular dementia and Alzheimer's, aged eighty. It is hard to remember the years before he started the long downward path, roughly fifteen years before he died. We noticed he was becoming irritable or 'irascible' as the professor suggested at St Mary's Hospital, Paddington on that dreadful day when he was finally diagnosed. This diagnosis, five years before he died, was given at the hospital where he had been born on 18 December 1926, to a young Welsh girl who was not to remain in his life for long.

Dick made plain his plans on that night we met. It was in the Blue Angel, Berkeley Street, Mayfair, in the heart of London's West End. He said something in such a way that I did not think what he was saying might include, or apply, to me: 'I plan to spend another five years in Hong Kong by which time the children will be coming up to boarding school age.' What was I to make of that?

I had invited this kind and generous lawyer from Hong Kong to dinner at the flat I shared in Teddington, a leafy London suburb, with my BOAC stewardess colleagues Sue, Laurie, Francine, and Moira. Previously, three of us had spent a wonderful holiday in Hong Kong in Dick's very nice duplex apartment, and I wanted to thank him. He was about to go on leave in Europe and had offered his home when he heard from his neighbours, Cathay Pacific pilots Peter, Bob, and Brian, of our imminent arrival.

So, there I was in Mayfair, dancing with this very handsome and sophisticated lawyer, after a failed dinner party, saved by two factors: the presence of Will Chalmers, a chief steward friend and hugely entertaining; and Dick's suggestion that he drive us in his Volvo P1800 to a night club. Sue's dinner had been inedible. The Hungarian goulash was full of hot chillies instead of regular peppers. As we entered the Blue Angel, Leslie Hutchinson or 'Hutch', the well-known black singer was at the piano playing 'Everything's Comin' Up Roses.' There was an aura of glamour and mystery around him, with his supposed friendships with Princess Margaret and Countess Mountbatten. The lights were low, and I was soon in Dick's arms. Will Chalmers remarked to Sue as we left the club, 'I hear wedding bells.'

Dick then became more certain of himself, more direct, as within minutes he invited me to join him for a trip to Paris or Copenhagen. Two weeks later we were in a glorious hotel in Elsinore near Copenhagen, and he asked me to marry him, though not before he had made sure I liked children. Now I realise that behind this spontaneous façade lay the cautious mind of a lawyer, and one that had experienced hurt and rejection. Dick might have seemed rash, but he trod carefully. He was something of an enigma, simple yet perplexing.

'The Catch of Hong Kong': that is how I heard him described by a lady living in Hong Kong soon after I arrived as a bride in 1962. He had led a dashing bachelor life in the Crown Colony but unusually chose to live in Sha Tin out in the countryside of the New Territories. This made him different. He never sought to keep up appearances. His choice of the girlfriends I heard about - when staying in his flat in Sha Tin before I met him - seemed to be mainly dancers. That is why I was surprised when the CPA pilot Bob Crockett said, 'You should meet Dick Dennis; he's just your type.' 'What, me?' I thought, 'A vicar's daughter?'

After he died, and we had been married for nearly 45 years, I decided to write a book starting with his early life in North China. It was a way of getting to know him and understand the man who held so much in. He had learned to do that very

Dick Dennis, my husband.

early on in his childhood. Throughout our marriage, until he became ill with smoking related diseases, he was in control. He was a kind and devoted husband and father, but the desire to control at times stood in the way of him maintaining a close relationship with his family.

There was so much to admire in Dick. I compare him to my great-great-grandfather, Thomas Dale. Both men were deprived of home-life early on with the disappearance of their mothers: Thomas by death; Dick by his mother giving birth to a daughter by another man, and subsequent divorce from his father. They were both awarded a place at Cambridge through determination and hard work and I feel great pride in all they achieved. Their children had a lot to live up to and were set fine examples.

Dick had two careers after serving in the navy from 1943-45. He was a lawyer in Hong Kong for eighteen years, followed by the same time as an executive in Rediffusion Television after we returned to England in 1969. After he retired at fifty-seven, he was not particularly active. The change from a dynamic leader to someone who seemed to be gradually withdrawing from life was sad and perplexing to me. He loved his sons and his daughters-in-law, and the arrival of each grandchild brought him enormous pleasure. There were seven when he died in 2007 and two more to come.

Dick seemed to want to do very little after he retired. Gardening was his main pleasure. Slowly his memory started to fade and our gardener, Ray Bullock, told me, 'Mr. Dennis is forgetting plant names.' That was the beginning of the person who had always been in control starting to fade and become someone else. His love of dogs remained with him until the end, along with his charm and good manners to those around him. The day before he died, in the Hospice of St John and St Elizabeth, he made sure the two friends who were with me had something to drink.

I managed to keep him out of hospital, except for emergencies, until the last five weeks of his life. As anyone knows who has cared for a family member with Alzheimer's or any other kind of dementia, a partner can feel lonely when living with someone no longer able to express emotions as they used to. At times this can be very hurtful. However, there were happy times too. With the help of two young men, Felix and Alvaro from Social Services, and a super, new wheelchair, Dick had plenty of local outings. I took him on holiday to friends In Spain and then to an apartment in Nice, not long before he died. Walks along the Promenade des Anglais were much enjoyed. The enjoyment was not always obvious. Everything becomes muted with a dementia sufferer. With Dick there were two exceptions: one being when I deprived him of a cigarette and he found a way of cadging one off a stranger when out with Felix; the other being the appearance of a family member, when Dick's face would light up with joy.

I was delighted we got to celebrate Dick's 80th birthday. Dick loved the ballet, so we went to see *Sleeping Beauty* at Covent Garden with his old friend from Hong Kong, Dr Kenneth Searle, and his wife. I had the usual battle at the interval to persuade him to return to his seat. He was insistent he would stay in the bar. There were many battles of this nature with Dick, testament to his strong personality. We also had a superb lunch party at a restaurant, just behind Bourdon Street in Bruton Place. Family and old friends joined us, and Dick was very happy seated between two very old girlfriends of mine from school and nursing training. The following day, the boys took us to the Savoy Grill. Dick had advanced dementia by then but loved every minute. His new three-piece, pin-striped suit, which I had struggled to get him to try on in John Lewis, looked very smart.

We were fortunate he did not have to go into a home. Our boys were adamant about this. Our three boys meant everything to him, but perhaps it was not until he had gone that they realised the full extent of his devotion. The title of my first book repeats Dick's words to our youngest son just before he died. James had thanked him for all he had done for them to which Dick replied, 'It was all I ever wanted.'

CHAPTER 17: EMILY RICHARDSON
Clever, Vivacious, and Amusing

What do we know about my great-great-grandmother Emily Richardson? Helena Pelham Dale's book contains a physical description of Thomas but not of her. Thomas' last will and testament mentions at least one portrait of her, which was passed on to Thomas Pelham. Both she and her oldest son, were Aries (like me), so I imagine she had the characteristics of being energetic, forceful, outgoing, and headstrong, often rushing into things without reflecting. She was born on 23 March 1803 and baptised on 19 April 1803 at St Michael's Church, Cornhill, where she would later marry Thomas Dale when she was only sixteen. Like her mother, Emily gave birth to many children – fifteen in total. Three of them died – Emily, Frances Josephine, and George Desborough - but in each case, the names were given to new babies who survived.

After their first son, Thomas Pelham Dale, was born in 1821, Emily gave birth to another son, James Murray Dale, on 22 July 1822 and he was baptised on 1 August at the church of St Mary Magdalene in East Ham, although the family was then living in Greenwich. A daughter, Emily Jane Dale, was born on 16 June 1824; Thomas baptised her himself on 14 July. He had also baptised Guildford Barker Richardson, then around seven years old, who was Emily's youngest brother, on 16 April that year. This Emily must have died in infancy, although thus far no record has been found of her death, as the Dales had another daughter, also named Emily Jane Dale, on 1 July 1827 in Beckenham. A son, Lawford William Torriano Dale was born on 20 February 1826. Two more daughters were born in Beckenham, in quick succession, Helen Hutton Dale in 1829 and Rose Anna Murray Dale. Then, two more children arrived, Clara Malcott Dale in 1832 and William Charles Dale in 1833.

When they lived in Beckenham, Emily helped Thomas with his teaching. Pupils – and their son Thomas Pelham Dale – remembered she could recite Walter Scott novels by heart and that she was a great encouragement. Thomas Pelham also remembered how she encouraged him with his love of science and helped him conduct scientific experiments at home. Her granddaughter Helena Pelham Dale described Emily as being 'clever, vivacious and amusing'. These must have been her father's words as she would not have remembered her grandmother herself.

Meanwhile, people were coming from far and wide to hear her husband preach, especially when he was at St Bride's, Fleet Street. Mrs Carr, who was a teacher at the parish school, wrote in her recollections that it was often impossible to get a seat in the church. It was she who described Thomas processing into the church, up the centre aisle, followed by his wife and twelve children. When the parish census was taken in 1831, there were 8,162 inhabitants of the parish but the church could only contain 1,500–2,000 at most.

Emily would have been kept very busy with parish duties as her husband's career progressed in the Church. Heavily pregnant, in the spring of 1835, she and the family moved into 65 Lincoln's Inn when Thomas was appointed as vicar of St Bride's. On 8 May that year, an entry appeared in the Parish Register detailing the baptism of Frances Josephine Dale, born on 29 March, another daughter. The ceremony was carried out by 'Thomas Dale, vicar of this parish.' The family residence was given as Grove Lane, Camberwell. Sadly, Frances died, aged a year and ten months, and she was buried at St Bride's. Her funeral on 28 January 1837 was conducted by Reverend Denis Kelly, Thomas's curate. Only a few days later, on 7 February 1837, Emily gave birth to another daughter. They named her Frances Josephine Dale and Thomas baptised her at St Bride's on 20 March that year. This girl survived. She was my paternal great-grandmother.

The *Champion* on 21 October 1838 reported that the wife of Reverend Thomas Dale, vicar of St Bride's, had given birth to her twelfth child. The baby was a boy, and they named him George Spence Desborough Dale. He was baptised on 12 November. James Murray Dale, Thomas and Emily's second son, had just secured articles of clerkship with Charles Fiddy of Serjeant's Inn, Fleet Street, and Thomas had to sign the documents for him. Sadly, baby George was taken ill suddenly and died on 19 December that year. Reverend Kelly again officiated at the burial at St Bride's on 22 December. This would have been a comfort to the family at what would have been a very sad Christmas. However, it was not long before Emily was pregnant again. A little boy arrived on 25 January 1840, and they named him George Spence Desborough Dale also.

Thomas soon made his mark at St Bride's – opening a new church (Holy Trinity, Gough Square) and opening two parochial schools. Funds had to be raised for all these enterprises and Emily threw herself into the process. This article appeared in the *London Evening Standard* of 20 May 1841:

Yesterday at noon a sale of useful and ornamental work took place at Radley's Hotel, Bridge Street, Blackfriars, in aid of the building fund of the above schools. The sale was under the patronage of her most gracious and most charitable Majesty, the Queen Dowager, her Grace the Duchess of Beaufort, the Right Hon. Lady Ashley, Lady Mary Farquhar and the Lady Mayoress. In consequence of the following letter addressed to Mr. Edkins, treasurer of the school, the large room of the hotel in which the sale took place was densely crowded with well-dressed persons of both sexes:–

Marlborough House, May 18

Sir, —I am commanded by her Majesty the Queen Dowager to signify to you her gracious intention of honouring the fancy sale tomorrow with her presence tomorrow (Wednesday) at 3 o'clock.

I am, Sir, your most obedient servant,

HOWE.

Three o'clock and four o'clock arrived, and much to the disappointment of the visitors, there was no indication of her Majesty's arrival. Messengers were dispatched to Marlborough House to ascertain the cause, whereupon it was discovered the letter was a forgery, though it bore the official seal. On inspection, it was clearly seen that the seal had been transferred from some other letter. The business of the sale, however, went on. The arrangement of the several works, particularly the fancy, in the different parts of the room, was extremely tasteful and had a very pleasing effect.

That which attracted most attention was a magnificent piece of embroidery sent by her Majesty, the Queen Dowager, part of which was said to be the work of her own fingers. The Reverend Thomas Dale, Vicar of St Bride's, with several other clergymen, assisted at stalls for the sale of moral and religious books and prints, many of which were purchased by the visitors. Mrs Dale's stall for the sale of fancy works obtained much patronage from the female portion of the company. Indeed, none of the fair *marchandes*, and they were many, had reason to complain of their wares being neglected.

The Lady Mayoress was very active during the day in making the show go off briskly and her ladyship was ably assisted by all the gentlemen of the Committee. The children of all the schools were admitted and their healthy, cleanly and interesting appearance induced many to make purchases in their behalf. The whole scene was enlivened by an excellent band and the delicacies of the refreshment room contributed in no small degree to give the whole affair a most pleasurable character.

I love this story about Emily, as being married to a such a stern and highly achieving man cannot have been easy. It is hard to imagine the heartbreak of burying one child at St

Bride's and having the next one, a namesake, baptised shortly afterwards, as happened to both a son and a daughter.

As the 1840s got under way, the older children started to fly the nest. Thomas and Emily's eldest son, Thomas Pelham Dale, went off to study at Sidney Sussex College, Cambridge in 1841. James Murray Dale had qualified as a solicitor. Another baby – a boy – arrived in July 1843 and was baptised at St Bride's, under the name Cecil Clare Marston Dale. The family had moved by then, to 35 New Bridge Street, Blackfriars. A final baby, Reginald Francis Dale, was born on 12 September 1845 and baptised at St Bride's on 10 October, by his father. The family address was given as the Residentiary House, St Paul's, although I am not sure that all the family moved in there. Lawford Torriano Dale had just started term at Trinity College, Cambridge. Thomas Pelham Dale had just finished at Cambridge, graduating as twenty-fifth 'Wrangler' (meaning that he was in twenty-fifth place in terms of marks for those in his year awarded a first-class undergraduate degree in Mathematics).

From a family perspective, the 1840s were busy years for the Dale family. Thomas Pelham Dale, the eldest child, by then a Clerk in Holy Orders and newly appointed as Rector of St Vedast's, was married on 7 October 1847, at St Mary's, Reigate, to Mary Francis. Their first child, Thomas Francis Dale, was born in August 1848, Thomas and Emily's first grandchild. Thomas and the rest of the family moved into no. 63 Russell Square, and he allowed the newly-weds to move into the house at Amen Court.

Built in Queen Anne's day, the house in Amen Court had rather a grand oak staircase and was full of timber. The London Evening Standard of 9 August 1848 carried a report to the effect that a fire had broken out on the second floor which soon spread to the third floor, its flames illuminating the whole of the City. The nursemaid attending Mary, who had only recently given birth, had accidentally set fire to the curtain around the bed with a lighted candle. There was speculation in the crowd that the baby had been burnt, but this was not the case. The page boy, who was deaf, was seen escaping over the neighbouring rooftops in his nightshirt and new livery hat. Considerable damage was done to the house and neighbouring properties and the house had to be rebuilt.

A happier event followed in a few months; on 30 January 1849, Thomas and Emily's daughter Helen Hutton Dale was married to John Cunliffe Pickersgill, a merchant. Thomas officiated at the ceremony, which was held at St Pancras New Church.

Then, Emily Jane Dale died on 7 April 1849, at home at 63 Russell Square, of a haemorrhage from a uterine polyp, a sudden cerebral effusion and general debility. Sarah Crow, their housekeeper, was with her when she died, and she registered the death a few days later. It was Holy Saturday. Notices of her death appeared in *Bell's Weekly Messenger and in the Atlas*. In the *Evening Standard,* she was referred to as Thomas's 'beloved wife'.

Emily's death would have left a tremendous hole at the centre of the Dale family. Their two youngest boys were so young: Cecil was not quite six; Reginald not quite four. William Charles Dale had just started work as a coffee merchants' clerk. Another daughter, Emily Jane Dale, married Charles Cotton Ferard of Ascot Place, Windsor, at St George's, Bloomsbury on 28 January 1851, with her brother, Thomas Pelham, officiating. When the 1851 census was taken, the family were at 63 Russell Square, with Sarah Crow, still their housekeeper, along with a nursemaid, a general maid, a cook, a nursemaid and a pageboy. At Gordon Square, nearby, Thomas's daughter Helen gave birth in 1850 to two children within the space of one year, Helen and John, and lost a baby daughter, Rose at the age of six weeks in 1852. We may not know much about Emily, but we do know she was 'clever, vivacious and amusing' and that she no doubt played a considerable role in the success of her remarkable husband.

CHAPTER 18: MY CHILDREN
Three Wonderful Boys

I love babies, and so did Ah Choi, our general *amah* (or maid) in Hong Kong in the 1960s. It was a race between us who would get to the cot first at the hint of a cry. It was obvious our boys would become very spoiled if we remained in Hong Kong, although unlike most Europeans I did not want a baby *amah*, preferring to have an active role in their childcare myself. Ah Choi was the common-law wife of our cook, Ah Kong. She was devoted to the boys and would carry first Matthew, then James around on her back. By the time she and Ah Kong came to us at Clifftop from Sha Tin, our oldest son Richard was already two and too big for that mode of transportation. He was soon riding his tricycle round and round the house, a Christmas present from Ah Kong and Ah Choi.

The time came for the boys to attend the Robins play group in Kowloon, so when each of them reached three, Dick drove them there, in his Volvo P1800, picking up other children along the way. There were no seat belts, of course. When Richard was five, he went on the school bus to Kowloon Junior. The bus stopped at the top of the rough unmade road which made its twisty way down to Clifftop, passing only one house on the way. He came home every day in time for lunch, and Ah Kong cooked calf livers and sheep brains for them amongst other 'delicacies'. The boys shuddered in later years when I told them they had eaten sheep brains.

Once we were back in England, Island Farm in Biddenden, Kent, where we lived from 1970 to 2004, was a wonderful place to bring up our three boys. Our house and garden were open to their many friends; the swimming pool and tennis court we installed in 1974/5 acted like a magnet in the summer. We hardly ever drove to the Kent coast as we were self-sufficient.

Trips to Maidstone for prep school uniform, and Tunbridge Wells for the dentist were about it, except for ferrying them round to parties until they could drive. Every Christmas they put on a play in which there was always a part for one of the four Labradors (Bruce, Rufus, Joseph and Jasper) that we had over the years. Richard wrote the plays and always played the 'baddie,' usually a German soldier.

The boys went to a local preparatory school in Cranbrook, known as Dulwich College Prep School (DCPS) or Coursehorn. The school had been evacuated during the war from Dulwich in London and had remained in Kent. I shared the school run with neighbours and our vicar's wife, Audrey Waite. Richard boarded from age eleven and Matthew from twelve to prepare them for Charterhouse in Surrey, their secondary, or public school. It was a sad day for James when Matthew started to board as he was going to be on his own. 'Who will help me with my homework?' he asked tearfully.

We had brought home a dachshund called Tuppet from Hong Kong, who was around in the early days of Bruce. Like all dachshunds, Tuppet did a lot of barking and terrified the Victoria Wine delivery man to the extent he would not come past the gate. The boys never forgave me for Tuppet's sudden demise: he was wearing a cardboard hood to stop him biting a sore on his back and as I reversed the car on the flagstones outside the house and drove off to Headcorn station to meet someone, I did not see him. James found him lying on the flagstones, and ran across the road to Paulette, telling her, 'I think Tuppet is dead.' I felt guilty for a long time.

Twice a year we had family holidays, with Dick driving the family estate wagon. In the summer we would head for a hotel on the Cote d'Azur or to the Dordogne for camping. Every winter it was skiing in the Alps. Although Dick did not ski himself, he took great pleasure in taking the boys to ski school and making sure they were enjoying themselves. I also joined the ski school but was far less successful than my sons. Over the years we visited Les Arcs, Flaine, Serre Chevalier, and Verbier, with various friends or relatives coming with us.

The Lake District, Scotland and the Yorkshire Moors were also included in our range of holidays, but the one the boys enjoyed most was when we flew to Kuala Lumpur in 1978. Two employees of Rediffusion accompanied us, Michael Bleecke and Tunku Mizan. At that time Dick was the CEO of Rediffusion Far East. After a night in Kuala Lumpar, we headed by road to the Taman Negara National Park, one of the world's oldest deciduous rain forests. To reach the park, we had a three to four-hour car journey followed by two to three hours by boat on the Taman river. As the river narrowed, we transferred to boats that were more suitable. We saw faces peering at us on the riverbanks. It was 1978 and the tourist industry was only just starting there. We stayed in government rest-houses with overhead fans and mosquito nets. I remember breakfast being served in a large hut, and endless toast arriving as it seemed no one had ever requested toast before. Dick carried our breakfast along a path back to our rooms, looking very alarmed when he saw a monkey was watching him closely and was about to swoop.

When back in Kent, camping in Hook Wood was a feature every summer. This was fifty acres of woodland purchased by Dick from the farmer, Martin Malony, who lived across the road from us. The trees were going to be cut down, so Dick came to the rescue. Each year he would ask Martin if we could use his tractor and trailer to take the camping gear, boys, dogs, plus any friends who might be around into the wood. One year it was the Newtons, Robin, Shandy, Gill and Mark, over from California.

As soon as they reached eighteen the boys would enjoy the local pubs - the Three Chimneys in Biddenden and the Bell in Smarden. They had a large circle of friends in Kent and East Sussex; at Dick's funeral in London in 2007, many of them came to pay their respects. They had fond memories of the

My three sons.

glorious Island Farm garden where swimming and tennis were enjoyed, and barbecues and parties held.

Dick was a great father to his sons. Each year he would also take them to the Cup Final at Wembley, made possible by the fact that Rediffusion and BET owned the stadium. Our boys were the envy of their prep school friends. I found it hard when they went off to Charterhouse; I missed them so much. Our thirty-four years at Island Farm were wonderful and the boys have very happy memories of growing up there. Dick's love of the country was passed on to his sons. We gave up the farm to settle in our Mayfair home in 2004, but after Dick died in 2007, the boys all left London to live in the countryside of Kent and Dorset. It was hard to leave Island Farm, but when Dick became ill, I knew I could not stay there with no boys and be isolated in the countryside while Dick struggled with dementia.

No parents are perfect, but Dick and I were united in the fact that our children needed love and security. The psychologist, John Bowlby, who developed the idea of 'attachment theory' wrote in his 1980 book *Loss, Sadness and Depression* (p.442) that 'Intimate attachments to other human beings are the hub around which a person's life revolves, not only when he is an infant or toddler or a schoolchild but through his adolescence and his years of maturity and on into old age.' We were not perfect parents but we both invested time in our sons.

Both Dick and I had been separated from our parents. For me it was being sent away for safety from London aged seven; Dick had the trauma of his mother disappearing when he was aged three, followed by a stepmother with whom he appeared to have no close attachment. Indeed, Dick had no family life after age twelve when he returned from North China in 1939 to boarding school. His father, the Chief of Police in the British Concession in Tientsin, stayed behind to cope with the worsening situation there following the start of the Second World War. Dick did not see him again for many years. If Dick were alive today, he would be happy to be surrounded by our family which includes three wonderful daughters-in-law and nine grandchildren.

Richard, the eldest of the boys, lives in Dorset and is his own boss. He has a company that deals in sports and TV.

He typically works from home and his London office twice a week, making frequent trips abroad. He is married to Lisa. They have two daughters and a son - Romilly, Eden and Hector – who are a credit to them. Being Dennises, dogs are an extremely important addition to the family - retrievers, and a dachshund, which reminds Richard of his Hong Kong childhood. There is also a horse for Romilly.

Matthew lives in Kent with his wife Suzie and their two boys, Jamie and George, and a gorgeous black Labrador, Wilbur, who has succeeded Cato, their beloved first dog. Jamie and George both left home for university, and Jamie is now working in Bristol, in air quality control. Matthew, like his younger brother James, is a lawyer. Both are partners in London law firms.

James lives with his wife Jane a short drive away. They have four children - Tom, William, Anna and Daisy – and live in a farmhouse that is reminiscent of Island Farm. They were a cat family, but finally Jane was won over to the idea of a Labrador puppy. Gracie arrived just after Christmas, the first female dog in the Dennis family. Needless-to-say, they are all captivated and she is a bundle of joy.

Whatever our shortcomings, Dick and I produced three wonderful sons: not just because of their academic prowess and successful careers, but because they are warm, loving and responsible human beings. I am enormously proud of all three of my sons and the choices they have made in life.

CHAPTER 19: DALE CHILDREN
Ritualist Controversy

The most famous, or infamous, of the Dale children was Thomas and Emily's firstborn, Thomas Pelham Dale (1821–1881). He was sentenced for 'Ritualism'. Part of his 'crime' was wearing Eucharistic vestments. He took the keys to his church with him to Holloway Prison.

His fame comes from his appointment as Rector of St Vedast's, Foster Lane, in 1847. In 1848, the *Mechanics Magazine* commented that the living was within the gift of the Dean and Chapter of St Paul's 'and therefore obtained for the young man through the paternal influence of the Canon himself.' The article went on to quote 1 Timothy 5:8, 'He that provideth not for his own, and especially those of his own house, hath denied the faith and is worse than an infidel.' At the time, Thomas Pelham was applying for the Gresham Professorship. He did not get the position, but the article did concede that he was 'a man of real ability'.

He was appointed as librarian at Sion College in 1852, a difficult task as it transpired. One of his predecessors, Henry Christmas, had been ejected from the post and questions had arisen over some of his acquisitions. The library was in a chaotic state and this was something Thomas Pelham managed to sort out, providing a useful working catalogue.

We have mentioned Thomas Pelham's early interest in science, and the discussions he used to have with his mother. He kept this up. He worked with John Hall Gladstone on what became known as the 'Gladstone and Dale Law'. They addressed the Chemical Society in 1865, explaining that Gladstone tended to carry out the experiments whilst Thomas Pelham worked on the mathematical side of their research. Their law was as follows:

When a substance is compressed or its temperature is altered, the density (ρ) alters, and this is accompanied by a corresponding variation in the refractive index (μ). The equation expressing this is:

$$\frac{\mu - 1}{\rho} = \text{constant}$$

St Vedast's is on the east side of Foster Lane, Cheapside. Thomas Pelham inherited a church with a history. Dedicated to St Vedast, Bishop of Arras, there has been a church on the site from at least 1170 until today. Thomas More grew up in nearby Milk Street, and Robert Herrick, the poet, was baptised in the church. St Vedast's was badly damaged by the Great Fire of London and was included in the list of churches that required reconstruction by Christopher Wren.

However, as Thomas Pelham's tenure got under way, London was changing. The population was migrating out of the centre and the City and into the suburbs, so that there was a 'day population' and a 'night population'. The coming of the railways had a considerable part to play, of course. We can see by contrast how his father's parish, not far from the City, had expanded to a level that was difficult to manage.

In his series of sketches published between 1860 and 1861 under the banner of 'The Uncommercial Traveller,' Charles Dickens wrote, 'These deserted churches remain like the remains of the old citizens who lie beneath them and around them, monuments of another age.' As a response, the Union of Benefices Act of 1860 was passed, which allowed City church sites to be sold to pay for new churches in the suburbs. St Vedast's was not one of them.

Thomas Pelham kept busy, learning Hebrew and Arabic. He helped his father with some of the pastoral work in the parish of St Pancras. As a result of poverty witnessed there, he set up, with Elizabeth Catherine Ferard (a relative by marriage of Emily) and one of his sisters, the North London Deaconess Institute in 1861. His idea was that there should be a home and organisation for women who did not have the calling to become nuns but wanted to devote their energies to charitable works.

An article in the *London City Press* of 16 May 1868 titled 'The Thin End,' reported:

> St Vedast, Foster Lane, is, it appears, to have a higher order of service than has hitherto prevailed. The Reverend T Pelham Dale, the Rector, son of Canon Dale, has announced that he will make an alteration which, he hopes, will render the services more attractive, not only to the parishioners but to others who may like to attend. He does not propose to adopt such high Ritualistic services as will overlay the doctrines of the Church but to avoid that slovenliness that is so often indulged in.

Again, in the *London City Press,* an article appeared on 16 January 1869 about a vestry meeting at St Vedast's, where Thomas Pelham stated his wish to improve the musical part of divine service at the church, explaining that he had started thinking about this one dull Sunday when the congregation was exceptionally small. He had no wish to have any other service 'except one to edify but at the same time he had no wish that the ear should be tortured by discordant sounds.'

The organist at the time was Mrs Ann Mounsey Bartholomew, who had been organist at St Vedast's since 1837. The churchwardens rallied around her and would not hear of her being removed. Thomas Pelham explained that she was an excellent player, but he had noted a marked change in her playing that Sunday. Mrs Bartholomew was well-known as an organist and composer and in fact continued to serve at St Vedast's for many more years.

Clearly, Thomas Pelham was 'treading on toes'. The churchwardens, whose appointment, by some sort of parochial and ecclesiastical quirk was not entirely – as Helena Pelham Dale relates – within Thomas Pelham's gift, included John Clifford Serjeant, a shoemaker from Gutter Lane, George Robert Bengough, a trunkmaker, James Horwood and Robert

George Morley. Helena Dale described vestry meetings as 'a modern substitute for the rack', explaining, 'If the Rector did not go, all sorts of votes for which he was considered responsible were passed; if he did, all the aggrieved ratepayers took their turn at insulting him.' One of the issues Thomas Pelham had was that the church charity funds were paid into Mr Serjeant's own bank account, which he considered improper. The officials, in his view, had large salaries and small duties, and the churchwardens seemed to think the money was theirs to spend as they wished.

St Vedast's was not in good repair, despite Thomas Pelham's constant requests for funds. The stone-paved aisles were full of dangerous pitfalls and curious holes, writes Helena Pelham Dale, while the rats that found their way into the church showed that there were openings in the vaults below. He was exasperated by the amount of money members of the vestry spent on elaborate dinners. In 1869, he closed the church for a few weeks for 'cleansing and refurbishment'

The Public Worship Regulation Bill began to gather pace. It was proposed by Archbishop William Campbell Tait, who had supported Thomas Pelham in the founding of the Deaconess Institute, to limit what he perceived as the growing ritualism and the Oxford Movement within the Church of England and to put down 'the Mass in Masquerade,' the latter being a phrase coined by Benjamin Disraeli, who was then Prime Minister and a supporter of the legislation, as was Queen Victoria.

For the background to this legislation, we must look further back into history, and to the change that took place in the relationship between the state and the Church of England from 1828 onwards. Laws that required members of municipal corporations and government office holders to receive communion in the Church of England were repealed, and legislation was passed that removed many of the restrictions on Roman Catholics. There was a fear that the Church of England might be disestablished and lose its endowments. Riots occurred at the church of St George-in-the-East, over changes the Vicar was making to worship there.

In 1873, the choir of the church of St Lawrence Jewry resigned 'en masse' when their new vicar wished to introduce certain changes with which they were not comfortable. They offered their services to Thomas Pelham, who accepted their offer and used the opportunity to alter the services at St Vedast's and to make a few 'alterations' to the furniture. He also began to use vestments, as opposed to the prescribed black gown, and to use the mixed chalice that Christmas. A letter published in the *Hastings and St Leonard's Observer* on 9 May 1874 from an anonymous correspondent in St Leonard's under the pen name 'Veritas' could almost have been penned by Thomas Pelham:

> Ritual, what is it? A Ritualist is commonly understood to mean one who pays more attention to the outward decency and order of God's service than has been ordinarily observed in English churches and who is doing a little against neglect, irreverence and sloth, both in outward and inward religion. Is any stir made because Evangelical parishes and those of the country parish are shut up from one week to another and certain services are entirely ignored? Let us take, for instance, a church not far from this town (we will not mention the name.) All there is to be seen there is four (once) white-washed walls, now dark green with damp and dirt, and cobwebs hanging from the ceiling a foot long, and the altar a common deal table covered with a red cloth, in tatters and smothered in dust.

The Public Worship Regulation 1874 allowed three male parishioners, an archdeacon or a church warden to serve on the bishop a representation that alteration to the fabric, ornaments or furniture of a church had been made without authority or that unlawful ornaments or vestments were being used in the church or burial ground. The churchwardens at St Vedast's seized their opportunity, almost as soon as the law was on the statue books. The bishop was then empowered to issue a monition, and if the vicar in question failed to comply, he could be imprisoned for contempt of court and a prison sentence imposed.

The issues the Vestry had with Thomas Pelham included the following: wearing an alb, chasuble and a stole; that he wore a biretta on entering and leaving the church; his back being towards the congregation when breaking the bread; using 'wafer' bread; elevating the patten and chalice above his head; elevating the offerings of the people; and the singing of the hymn 'Agnus Dei'. Enough was clearly enough in July 1875, when the entire congregation of St Alban's, Holborn processed one Sunday down Newgate Street and were welcomed into St Vedast's as their vicar had been suspended for ritualistic practices, with candles on the altar and Thomas Pelham emerging from the sacristy, in his vestments with his son Arthur Murray Dale, similarly arrayed, to take the service.

Thomas Pelham's was the first case to appear before Lord Penzance under the new Act. On 12th November 1876, John Jackson, Bishop of London, enforced an inhibition from the Court of Arches and instructed Thomas Pelham not to take any more services; the bishop took them himself for a while. However, there were technical issues with the prosecution, and Thomas Pelham began to take services again. By Christmas 1878 he was engaging in all his former practices and, after further lengthy proceedings, judgment was obtained against him in the Court of Arches on 28 October 1880. The *Penny Illustrated Paper* made a comment, to the effect that Reverend Dale took no more notice of Lord Penzance's orders than if they came from the *Pirates of Penzance*, but what happened next could no longer be ignored.

At half past seven on the evening of Saturday 30 October, the court tipstaff turned up at Thomas Pelham's home in Ladbroke Gardens, Notting Hill and took him away in a cab. A notice appeared on the church door the next day to the effect that in consequence of the Reverend Pelham Dale having been confined in prison 'for conscience's sake,' there would be no further services until further notice. Thomas Pelham took the key with him and the churchwardens had to break in through one of the windows. They barricaded themselves inside the church, in case 'any of Reverend Dale's supporters tried to take over'. Thomas Pelham did suggest that Arthur Murray could stand in for him in his absence, but this overture was rejected by the bishop.

His arrest caused a furore and there were demands for his release from many quarters; Arthur Murray Dale, wrote furious letters to *The Times*. The *Uxbridge and West Drayton Gazette* of 13 November 1880 reported that Arthur Murray had addressed a meeting of the English Church Union and had told them that his father's imprisonment was 'a blot on the fair fame of England' and that he trusted that Englishmen would demand justice and fair play. His family were able to visit him in gaol although two of his sons were serving overseas with the army – Charles Lawford Dale in the West Indies and Thomas Francis Dale as an army chaplain in Bombay. Thomas Pelham was treated kindly and given permission to walk in the grounds, but he had begun to suffer from attacks of giddiness. He was released on bail on Christmas Eve 1880 and freed altogether in January 1881. Not long after that, Thomas Pelham was offered the living of Skuthorpe-cum-Aswardby, near Spilsby in Lincolnshire, a parish of 126 souls. Arthur Murray Dale had recently been appointed curate there. Thomas Pelham had to agree not to make any changes to the practice of worship there. He moved into the Rectory with his wife, two unmarried daughters and a cook, a parlour maid, and a groom. The Church Association, which had supported the churchwardens in their case against him, continued to chase Thomas Pelham for costs, excited by the report that he was 'possessed of considerable landed property in Kent'.

Not long ago, I attended the church of St Mary-le-Strand and had the pleasure of meeting a man after the service, who, when I mentioned where I had been in the morning (to St Pancras's New Church where Thomas Dale was Vicar) and why, he exclaimed, 'Thomas Pelham Dale: imprisoned for ritualism!' This man's name is Peter Maplestone, and his book on the church of St Mary-le-Strand was published recently. I was bewildered on two counts: first, I thought Peter was talking about Canon Dale; and second, how on earth did he have this information, and why? He replied that he was 'a sad person who studied the history of the clergy'. 'What is your day job?' I asked, and it turns out he works for the Treasury. He was very interested to hear of my connection through Canon Dale's oldest son Thomas Pelham, Rector of St Vedast's from 1847 until his imprisonment for Ritualism in 1880. I have also visited St Vedast's. The black and white tiles of the main aisle of the church are stunning and are like those Christopher Wren incorporated into his design for another of his churches connected to the Dales, namely St Bride's, Fleet Street, known as 'the journalists church'. When I visited, I could imagine my great-great-grandfather walking up the aisle in a packed church for Sunday service accompanied by Emily his wife, with a dozen children behind them. I thought of three of their children being buried there with the next three who followed being baptised there and given the same names.

The Dale family came under the ritualist spotlight again when Arthur Murray Dale, then stipendiary curate in Chiswick under his uncle, Lawford Torriano Dale, was, according to the *Belfast Newsletter* of 31 March 1888 formally received into and conditionally baptised into what the article described as 'the apostate church of Rome' by the Reverend Reginald Tuke. As might be imagined, this did not go down at all well and the Protestant Alliance made a formal complaint to the Bishop of London. His uncle wrote to the papers to explain that Arthur Murray had indeed been formally received into the Roman Catholic Church 'whilst in a weak state of health' but that he was assured that his nephew's heart was not with the Church of Rome and that he would continue his ministry within the Church of England. An earlier article in the *Middlesex Independent* of 3 March 1888 under the headline 'True Colours' sheds further light; it appeared that several members of the congregation were received at the same time, including Miss Rawson, the organist.

Reverend Tuke was part of the Oxford Movement and had been a vicar in Soho before being received into the Catholic Church. He had set up a monastery in the East End of London and when he 'converted' Arthur, he was the priest at Our Lady of Grace and St Edward in Chiswick. It seems Arthur Murray had second thoughts – the 1902 obituary of Miss Rawson, who was received alongside him, intimates that he was under pressure from his relatives. This letter was read out to the congregation of St Mary Magdalene, Chiswick on 9 March: 'Dear Friends, please do not enter into any controversy about my religious opinions. Whatever I may have done, I am not now a Roman Catholic, but a clergyman of the Church of England.' The matter was at an end, or so it seemed.

Thomas Pelham Dale died on 19 April 1892 at the Rectory in Sausthorpe of heart disease. The point is made in various articles about Thomas Pelham that this was the eleventh anniversary of the death of Benjamin Disraeli, one of the supporters of the Public Worship Regulation Act. Thomas Pelham is buried on the eastern side of the graveyard. The *Lincolnshire Chronicle* of 22 April 1892 reported, 'During his ministration there his devotion to the work of the parish and his quiet and unassuming manner endeared him to his parishioners and all the residents in the neighbourhood.'

It was Thomas Pelham's daughter, Helena Annette Pelham Dale, who brought out *The Life and Letters of Thomas Pelham Dale* a couple of years later, in 1894. It was published by George Allen, Ruskin's publisher. Helena never married. The reviews suggest that there was an undertone of bitterness about the way her father had been treated and they also reveal that she ended up doing most of the work on it herself, when it had originally been planned that her brother (presumably Arthur Murray) would help her.

What became of Arthur Murray? He stayed on as curate at Chiswick for a while, becoming chaplain to an Anglican Benedictine order in Twickenham, who had set up in a house donated to them by his late father, and on Tuesday 26 June 1894, at what the newspapers commented was the unusually early time of 9am, married Mary Boscawen at St Thomas's Church, Regent Street, London. Mary was the daughter of the late 6th Viscount Falmouth. The reception took place at her family's London home and they had their honeymoon in Dores, near Inverness. Shortly after that, Arthur was offered the living at Sneinton, Nottinghamshire and he stayed there until 1902, when he became curate again, this time to Canon Murray (another member of the Oxford Movement) at Chislehurst. Canon Murray may have been a distant relative; it will be recalled that Arthur Murray's great-grandmother, Mary Richardson (née Barker) descended – as did Canon Murray - from the Murrays of Blair Castle.

Arthur and Mary did not have children. Mary died on 21 January 1916, at the Bailey's Hotel in South Kensington, suddenly and of a heart attack. Her funeral took place at Mereworth Church, her brother's family home being nearby. She left her estate – over £12,000 – to Arthur.

Under the headline 'Notable Convert,' an article appeared in the *Wicklow People* of 15 November 1924 to the effect that Arthur Murray Dale, well-known High Church clergyman, had been received into the Catholic Church, at a ceremony in Rome at the Private Chapel of the Pontifical Ecclesiastical Academy. He was received by Monsignor Barton Brown of London, confirmed by the Archbishop of Colossae and afterwards had an audience with the Pope.

On 16 April 1927, an article appeared in the *West Middlesex Gazette,* reporting on the funeral of 'Father Dale' at the church of Our Lady and St Joseph, Hanwell. The Mass was taken by his old friend, Monsignor Barton Brown. Many Catholic clergy attended but not, it would appear, any representatives of the Dale family. The chief mourner was identified as Lord Falmouth, a relative of his late wife. The Mass was also attended by Cardinal Bourne, Archbishop of Westminster, who pronounced the absolution at the bier. Arthur Murray's stole and biretta were placed on the coffin. Arthur's estate – he left over £9,000 – was dealt with by Monsignor Barton-Brown and Austin Hugh Handel, gentleman, who subsequently adopted the name Austin Hugh Handel-Dale.

It is curious that none of the Dale family – we do not know of the connection between Arthur and Austin Handel-Dale, who was born in 1906 - were counted among the mourners. Arthur Murray's two brothers were of course dead – Lieutenant-Colonel Charles Lawford Dale of Her Majesty's 1st West India Regiment in 1898 (in the York Hotel in Lambeth Road) and Thomas Francis Dale in Hampshire in 1923. Charles Lawford had married an Irish girl in Guyana, but they did not have children and she went to live with relatives in Birkenhead after his death. Thomas Francis Dale was estranged from his family although it was his son, Thomas Cyril Dale, who also went on to become a vicar, who was in possession of many of the family papers and who undertook a lot of genealogical research. However, Arthur Murray's sisters were all still alive.

Thomas Pelham Dale probably attracted the most attention of all the Dale children; the scholarly theologian who may at the outset simply wanted to try and make St Vedast's more attractive as a church, in view of the exodus from the City and the dwindling congregation. However, he was one of fifteen children (of whom twelve survived). What happened to the others?

Next in age to Thomas Pelham was James Murray Dale, born in 1822 and known to the family as 'Jem'. We have mentioned that he was articled as a solicitor to Charles Fiddy of

Serjeant's Inn. Exercised perhaps by the discussions that would have been taking place at home about how best to manage the burgeoning parish of St Pancras, he wrote *The Clergyman's Legal Handbook and Churchwardens' Guide*. It was published in 1869, with another of his brothers, Cecil, a barrister, named as editor. James also wrote a book in 1871 titled *Legal Ritual, the Judgments Delivered by the Dean of the Court of Arches and the Privy Council in the Case of Martin v. Mackonochie*. Reverend Mackonochie was Rector of St Alban's in Holborn and Thomas Pelham offered the congregation 'sanctuary' during the time of Father Mackonochie's suspension.

James Murray married Ann Eliza Norris in 1851 in Debenham, Suffolk. They had a large family and lived in Lee, near Blackheath. James died in 1877 at Rowley House, Aldeburgh, Suffolk. One of James' grandsons was Cousin Geoffrey, the Reverend Geoffrey Gunnell Newman who taught W.H. Auden at St Edmund's school in Hindhead, Surrey when he was a teacher and chaplain there.

The next of Thomas and Emily's sons was Lawford William Torriano Dale, who was born in 1826. The name Lawford comes from Emily's great-grandmother, Anne Lawford, the wife of John Malcott, 'citizen and mason of London'. I am not sure about 'Torriano'; there is clearly a family connection somewhere as Mr Torriano is mentioned in a letter to Thomas Dale from Thomas Pelham.

Lawford was educated at the Merchant Taylors' School and Trinity College, Cambridge. He was ordained a priest in 1850 and was curate in his father's parish from 1849 until 1857, when he became Vicar of Chiswick, a position he held until his death. With his wife, Fanny Dixon, Lawford had fifteen children; all but the last one, Christopher William (who died in early infancy in 1881) survived.

Like his brother, Lawford also had accusations of being too High Church. Having Arthur Murray Dale, his nephew and curate, received into the Catholic Church during his tenure probably did not assist and there were reports in the *West London Gazette* about his daughters having been received as well. However, any detractors were eventually won over by his tireless work within the parish. Dale Street in Chiswick is named after him. The *Acton Gazette* reported on 6 May 1898 that his parish included a large part of the slums of Chiswick and that his work for 'the indigent, the vicious and the ignorant' was beyond praise. Lawford also wrote the hymn tune 'Chiswick'.

Two of his daughters became nuns. Agnes Adela Dale became Mother Mary Beata of the Sisters of Sion and died in Sale, Victoria, Australia in 1947. Margaret Agatha Dale was in 1939 a choir nun at St Mary's Abbey in East Bergholt, a Benedictine order. It seems that another of Lawford's children, Edgar Lawford Dale, was received into the Catholic Church in later life.

Perhaps exhausted by all the childbearing, Fanny Dale left Lawford in 1887 and moved to Hillside Street, Hythe, Kent, taking Clement Pelham Dale, one of their sons, with her. Another son, Herbert Dixon Dale, became vicar of Hythe, and three unmarried daughters (Lilian, Grace, and Cicely) moved down with them. Fanny died a year or so before Lawford, of a burst blood vessel in the brain. Her body was brought back to Chiswick for burial.

When Lawford died, other than several specific bequests, he left most of his estate to his unmarried daughters, although he cut the two who had become Roman Catholic nuns out of his will, with the stern admonition that any daughter who was also thinking of taking the same route would meet a similar fate.

Herbert Dixon Dale, his son, who became Vicar of Hythe, did marry – late in life – but had no children. He narrowly escaped death on 25 May 1917, when Gotha bombers, unable to find their London targets due to thick cloud, turned towards the Channel ports and dropped bombs on Hythe and Folkestone. Herbert and his wife were chatting in the church yard – I have often walked up the hill there with Debby – to Daniel Stringer Lyth, the verger, when Daniel was struck in the thigh by a piece of shrapnel which severed his femoral artery and eventually killed him. Herbert was saved by a tobacco tin which was in his pocket and deflected the metal.

The next child was Emily Jane Dale, born in 1827. She married Charles Cotton Ferard, of Ascot Place, Winkfield, Berkshire, who was a barrister. It was Charles's younger sister, Elizabeth Catherine Ferard, who set up the North London Deaconess' Institution with Thomas Pelham Dale, and is remembered as a saint in certain parts of the Anglican communion on 3 July or 18 July. Charles, Emily's husband, inherited Ascot Place in around 1850 and became Lord of the Manor. It would have been a magnificent place for a young couple to start their married life. Charles and Emily are thought to have laid out the pleasure gardens and she is described in various newspaper articles as being very 'musically accomplished' and there are reports in the local newspapers of her organising concerts to raise money for local causes.

Emily and Charles had ten children – the youngest boy was born in Vevey in Switzerland. One daughter, Emily Rose, married Sir Walter Armstrong, British art historian and author and director for many years of the National Gallery in Dublin. Two of the boys went into the Indian Civil service - Henry Cecil Ferard, became a magistrate and Collector at Allahabad and John Edward Ferard a Senior Clerk.

Charles, described after his sudden death from an aneurysm in 1886, was described as 'an indefatigable magistrate and an ardent churchman'. Emily died on 8 September 1899 at 5 Shorncliffe Road, Folkestone, where she was staying with one of her unmarried daughters.

Helen Hutton Dale was born in 1829 in Beckenham. She was the first of the Dale girls to marry – just a few months before her mother's death. She married John Cunliffe Pickersgill, a London merchant of the firm Pickersgill and sons and the proprietor of large-landed estates in the county of Yorkshire. He served for about six weeks as Conservative member of parliament for Bewdley, but his election was overturned as certain voting irregularities were identified. John died in Guy's Hospital in 1873, following an accident on a train crossing at Caterham. Helen was left with a large and still young family. Their youngest child, Millicent, was around a year old and further tragedy was to occur, with the death that November of their twelve-year-old daughter, Margaret Emily, just after probate had been taken out of John's will. Happier times would follow when, on 14 January 1875, her eldest daughter Helen married Charles Thomas Farquhar Hodgkinson, a Captain in the Royal Navy, although shortly afterwards they emigrated to the United States.

Not long after that, Helen moved to Lamorbey House near Dartford, which she rented. Her eldest son John died there in 1879 of acute typhoid fever. She then moved to the Great Hermitage, in Higham (near Gravesend) where, in 1891, she is shown as living with various of her children and her nephews and nieces. There was a newspaper report to the effect that there had been a burglary at the Hermitage, where valuable family jewellery was stolen. She then moved to Northwood Hall, Middlesex where she died on 14 November 1914, having outlived several of her children (she gave birth to seventeen altogether).

Rose Ann Murray Dale was born in 1830 in Beckenham. She did not marry and accompanied her father to Therfield and then settled in London, described on various censuses as a fund-holder. She died in 1890 at 73 Gower Street (these were, according to the *Evening Standard*, 'superior apartments') and was the only one of the Dale children to be buried beside him in Highgate Cemetery. She left an estate of around £5,000.

Clara Malcott Dale, who also never married, was born in 1833. She died in 1905 in Oxford, also leaving an estate of around £5,000. Probate of her estate and of her sister Rose was dealt with by their younger brother, Reverend Reginald Francis Dale.

William Charles Dale was born in 1834 in Camberwell. He married Priscilla Brunning, at St Martin's Ludgate on 1 July 1858; he was a stockbroker. News of their marriage – unlike those of the other Dale children - did not appear in the papers. Priscilla was seventeen and the daughter of an artist and scene painter, William Allen Brunning. Her father had died in 1850, in his early thirties – Pieter Van der Merwe of the National Maritime Museum has written about his work, describing him as someone who died too young to fulfil his early promise.

Priscilla's younger brother, Henry Calcott Brunning, also went on to work for the stock exchange but he became a very wealthy man and a patron of the arts. When Henry died, in 1907, he left his money to Priscilla and any of her daughters who had not 'embraced the Roman Catholic faith or entered any other religious order'. This may have been directed at one particular niece, Muriel Constance Dale, an Anglican nun with the Sisters of the Poor. She became a Roman Catholic in 1908. In fact, the only one of William and Priscilla's children to marry was Lionel Newman Egerton Dale, but he and his wife did not have children. William died in 1888 in Worthing and there is no sign of his having made a will and his death was not reported in the newspapers. In his father's will, he was left £200 and a silver salver.

The next Dale child was Frances Josephine Dale, my great-grandmother, about whom much has already been said.

Then George Spence Desborough Dale was born in 1840. As previously mentioned, his birth was not registered centrally, although he was baptised. Thomas and Emily had lost two children in quick succession, one of them also having been named George Spence Desborough Dale. George, after studies at King's College, London, passed the examinations for the Indian Civil Service, and, in 1861, was appointed as Magistrate and Collector at Mirzapore. On 7 September 1865, he married

Alice Augusta Davis, 'aged 18 and a half' at Trinity Church in Allahabad. Alice had been born in Lahore. George died on 22 March 1889 of gunshot wounds. In a publication known as *Homeward Mail from India, China and the Far East,* this piece appeared on 13 April 1889:

> A gloom has been cast over our little station by the sad death of the popular Magistrate and Collector of Mirzapore, George S D Dale. It appears that the unfortunate gentleman had been suffering from some time past with insomnia and the people of the station had noticed that a change had come over him, thought there was not the slightest apprehension that he was in any way mentally affected. On Thursday evening, Mr. Dale retired to rest as usual, there also being in the bungalow Mr. Berkeley, our new District Superintendent of Police, and several other friends.

> Early yesterday morning, the chowkidar heard a report, but did not seem to think there was anything wrong, as Mr. Dale had been in the habit of coming into the compound at various hours to shoot pariah dogs. The man, proceeding on his usual round, came across the body of Mr. Dale lying apparently lifeless in the garden. He at once raised an alarm and the body was taken into the house, where it was found that Mr. Dale had been shot with a Derringer which he kept in his bedroom. Death must have been instantaneous. An examination of the deceased gentleman's sleeping quarters showed that he had taken a few drops of laudanum, no doubt to induce sleep. It is quite possible that he came across his death accidentally.

> Frequently, just before his death, he had spoken of the appointment he had received as officiating Commissioner of Fyzabad and had expressed himself much pleased at his promotion. He was extremely popular with all who knew him, and his death is greatly deplored by Europeans and natives alike and commiseration for his widow and orphans is general and heartfelt. The body was sent to Allahabad for internment in the cemetery there.

Another publication, *Colonies and India,* described him as 'an excellent public servant and a thoroughly honest, kindly and cultivated English gentleman'. George was buried on 23 March, at Holy Trinity, Allahabad, where he and Alice had married. They had four children – George Arthur Dale, who became a Brigadier in the Indian army, Bertram Cecil Dale, Norah Frances Dale (who never married and became a midwife,) and Edith Mary Dale (who married Clifford High Douglas and became an engineer and the first woman to fly in an experimental bomber aircraft.)

Cecil Clare Marston Dale was born in 1843. He went to Jesus College, Cambridge, where he studied Mathematics, and then he trained as a barrister at Lincoln's Inn. He was called to the Bar in 1868 and is described as 'an Equity draftsman and conveyancer'. Cecil was the author of various books, including *A Practical Treatise on the Law of Trusts*. Cecil married Harriet Isabella Lanham in 1881 at St Andrew's, Holborn. They did not have children and Harriet died in 1892. In later life, Cecil lived with his niece, Violet (one of William Charles Dale's daughters) at Sussex Lodge in Foots Cray. He left her his money when he died in December 1918.

Reginald Francis Dale, the youngest of Thomas and Emily's children, was born in September 1845. He and Cecil would scarcely have remembered their mother. Reginald was educated at the Blackheath Proprietary School. He got an Open Mathematical scholarship to Queen's College Oxford in 1863 and took an Honours degree in Mathematics and Classics. For a while, he was a master at Westminster School, then he took Holy Orders and was vicar of Bletchingdon, Oxfordshire until 1899. He then became a mathematical lecturer at Keble College, Oxford. He was an accomplished musician and studied for another degree in Music. Like his older brother Lawford, Reginald composed hymn tunes: 'St Petrox' and 'St Catherine' were both used in *Hymns Ancient and Modern*. He also co-wrote *A Musical Primer for Schools* with Reverend John Troutbeck, a fellow Master at Westminster, and this was published in 1876. Like his other older brother Thomas Pelham, Reginald kept up after university with his scientific interests and became a Fellow of the Royal Astronomical Society. Reginald died from a weakness of the heart in November 1919.

There is no doubt that the Dale children were people of extraordinary ability and many achievements but perhaps this is no surprise given their remarkable parents, Thomas and Emily. I am enormously proud to be counted among their number.

CHAPTER 20: GLOBE-TROTTING
Exploring the World

After Dick died, I found myself alone, really for the first time since before I got married. By then my three boys all had their own lives. In the final chapter of this book, I describe in detail what was a difficult time for me and how, although it was not easy, I found myself again. One of the things I eventually found the confidence to do - and have enjoyed enormously since - was to travel, sometimes alone, sometimes with a friend or two. It has greatly enriched my life. There is no way I could describe all the incredible journeys I have made, but I have selected five to describe here briefly: my two visits to India, my two trips to China, and my holiday in Australia – all a long way from my upbringing in Essex, Herefordshire, and Buckinghamshire.

In 2008, my sister-in-law Valerie Charrington suggested I accompany her to North-West India. I was about to start my MA but did not want to turn down an invitation like this, so was prepared to miss the first week at City University. Val and I flew to Calcutta, arriving at 5 a.m. The memory of the drive from the airport to our hotel remains in my mind. I had been to Delhi briefly with Dick to visit the Taj Mahal when he was on a business trip, but I was not prepared for Calcutta, with people living on the streets. The hotel was '3-star' (but should have been '2-star' judging by the plumbing in the bathroom) and there were photos of Felicity Kendal and her family adorning the walls of the reception area and dining room, since they were an acting family in India during Felicity's childhood. We only had two nights there and did what sightseeing we could but had no chance to recover from our flight due to lack of sleep from the all-night traffic and tooting of horns. From the airport, we flew to Siliguri, a place we had never heard of, and the only memorable thing was the colour of the hotel swimming pool: it was green.

Our guide and driver collected us after one night there and we were happy to be on our way after a poor start to our trip. Everything improved as we drove towards Gangtok, in beautiful Sikkim, Kalimpong in West Bengal, and lastly Darjeeling, famous for its tea plantations. The scenery was wonderful, but the driving was quite terrifying. We often came across landslides on the road, but our driver seemed to have no fear of oncoming traffic. A highlight of this part of the trip was getting up at 2 a.m. in Darjeeling when the guide rang us to tell us this was a good time to see Mount Everest. We also had a superb visit to the tea-growing area. Having first witnessed the poverty on the streets of Calcutta and the skeletal dogs and ponies which pulled the carts for sightseers, it was a relief to get out into the stunning countryside of Sikkim and West Bengal. I was brought back to London while in Darjeeling: my MA course at City had begun and I was asked to write a few descriptive paragraphs on the topic of rain. Val helped me. I had also begun reading what turned out to be my favourite, creative, non-fiction book on our reading list: *In Cold Blood* by Truman Capote.

We left for Delhi from Darjeeling from where we went to Shimla by train. It was the summer capital of India during the British Raj as it is cool up there in the mountains. The Viceroy's palace is what I remember, along with the Victorian architecture and the snow-capped mountains. There was a book shop where I bought my first Dostoevsky: *The Idiot*. We also saw a Hindu wedding party. It passed us in a quiet street, with the bridegroom riding a white horse. There was music to accompany the bridal pair and the whole thing was a great spectacle. I was so glad Val encouraged me to make that trip. It did me the power of good.

I visited India again in 2019. My middle son Matthew suggested I did India 'in style', as opposed to doing it on the cheap.

He urged me to contact his friend, a travel agent. It was a very different experience from 2008 with Val. Indeed, it was luxury personified, by which I mean staying in 5-star hotels and at the occasional summer palace, formerly belonging to a maharaja. At the same time, we felt safe to try street food and to enjoy local experiences, such as a short journey on a local train with open doors. It is safer for the elderly to travel in a group in India. Our guide was well educated, and we learned a great deal from him - about the caste system, the different styles of dress depicting where the individual came from, and religion. He even taught us how to meditate. We congregated in my hotel room near the end of our trip. I realised that our guide could cope with the most difficult situations, and clients, by meditating. In Jaipur the previous week, I was tired and wanted to return to our hotel rather than see another temple. He suggested I travel on a tuk tuk (or 'auto-rickshaw'). It was the worst twenty minutes of my entire year. Our hotel was out in the suburbs and my neck has never been the same since being jolted around at breakneck speed. Our guide seemed unconcerned. I felt that his calm attitude was on this occasion misplaced. I wanted sympathy.

I was not as horrified by the poverty as I had been in Calcutta, since I saw the dignity of those who worked in what appeared to us as squalid and hopeless conditions. I am thinking of the Dhobi Ghat in Mumbai, the open-air laundromat. The washers, known as 'dhobis', work in the open to clean clothes and linen from Mumbai's hotels and hospitals. It was constructed in 1890. We were taken there one late afternoon when the dhobis had finished work for the day. Children were playing with each other in a playground outside the school. There was not a mobile device in sight, in contrast to seeing children in the UK playing on their phones and other gadgets. Shoes were lined up outside the apartments where they lived. It was clean and orderly. I came home from that trip with a better understanding of India, albeit superficial, and how it it works. Religion is a central part of their lives. Living with very little in the sense of material goods does not always mean misery.

Back in 2009, since I was writing a memoir at City, I felt I had to visit China. Dick had spent part of his childhood in Tientsin (now Tianjin) from 1935-39. The travel agent I went to see in London was not confident that I would find anything from the 1930s in Tianjin, 'The Chinese knock everything down,' he said. Luckily for me, he was wrong.

I flew to Hong Kong and, after spending a day or two there, left on the night train to Shanghai. This was an exciting experience as when we lived in Hong Kong in the 1960s no one could cross the border into China from the New Territories (except those with a special visa or permits, certain business-people, and many Chinese at the Lunar New Year). The night train was fantastic, and I felt a thrill of excitement as the train passed over the border from Hong Kong into China. As we headed north, the landscape, which was sub-tropical, gradually became less green and lush. The journey took nineteen hours, and I had a good night's sleep - apart from an uproar outside when a young, drunk Cantonese woman was dragged along the corridor by her feet back to her cabin by the stewards, with much shouting in Cantonese.

The next step was arriving in Shanghai and being met by a guide and driver after a good English breakfast was served to me in my cabin. A visit to the famous restaurant M on the Bund remains in my mind and I was dazzled by a tall building with '1949' in bright lights written on it, a reminder of the revolution when Mao Zedong came to power and the Nationalists fled to Taiwan.

I flew to Beijing after two days, and there had a wonderful guide called Shane, who took me to all the famous places, such as Tiananmen Square (although no questions were answered about 1989) and the Forbidden City. The city was getting ready for a visit from President Obama. What I really wanted to see, however, was the Fox Tower where the body of a murdered British girl had been dumped in January 1937. Dick's father was recalled from his post as Chief of Police in the British Concession of Tientsin to help solve the crime (a story described in Paul French's 2011 book *Midnight in Peking*). From Beijing, our guide and driver drove me to Tianjin via the Great Wall, on what was their first visit to Tianjin. Snow was on the ground early that year. It was November and I was glad of the thick, quilted coats I had bought in Beijing.

Tientsin had been a 'treaty port'. These opened-up foreign trade, permitting foreign legations in Beijing which effectively legalised the import of opium. I felt emotional being in the city where Dick had spent the years 1935–39 with his father and stepmother Virginia. He had attended the French Consulate School, and we managed to find that in the French quarter of the city, not far from the British Concession. All his lessons were in French and I wondered how, as a nine-year-old from London, he had adapted to that. His fluent French enabled him to have many French clients when working as a lawyer in Hong Kong from 1952 to 1969.

My guide took me to the British Concession the next morning and I could not believe how wrong the travel firm in London had been in telling me that I would not find anything of historical interest there. There I was in Munan Road (formerly Hong Road) and it was end-to-end English-style houses built in the 1920s and '30s. I could have been in a leafy London suburb but for the bicycles parked outside and the washing hanging for all to see and indicating that more than one family lived in each house. There was a preservation order on the front of all the houses. One more thing made me realise I was in a Chinese city and not in Richmond, Surrey: the rag and bone man (or 'peddler') on his bicycle, was calling out his wares not in English but in Mandarin. It was wonderful; I could at last feel a link with Dick's past.

I so enjoyed my visit to China that the following year I visited again. This time I travelled to Tianjin from Beijing alone and by bullet train. Shane, my guide from 2009, took me to the huge station (built in preparation for the 2008 Olympics) and I was thankful he was there. Otherwise, I felt I would never have found the right train. There were no signs in English. This was not Hong Kong where the taxi drivers speak English and it is easy for tourists to get around, although I understand this is less the case now since the handover to China in 1997.

On this second trip to China, I saw far more of Beijing with Shane. I also had a great experience meeting a friend of a Hong Kong friend at the Red Capital Club. We arranged to meet at 7:30 p.m. and I left my hotel by taxi, travelling through the smart area of the embassies and consulates. My taxi driver then stopped. It was dark and I had to walk up a quiet alley to the famous restaurant favoured by Mao Zedong and Deng Xiaoping. A limo with a red flag on it was used to ferry Chinese leaders around the city sites outside the award-winning Red Capital Club's hutong courtyard. It was dark and mysterious inside, with the red theme continuing and 1950s memorabilia and furniture. The food was reputedly the best 'Zhongnanhai cuisine'. I wish I had made notes of what we ate.

On my second visit to Tianjin, I was met by a member of the British Council, a charming Chinese man, and his wife. This was arranged for me by my friend Professor Maurozio Marinelli who oversaw a project at Bristol University on 'Tianjin under Nine Flags' on the topic of the city being under nine foreign-controlled concessions between 1860 and 1945. After seeing the old racecourse where Dick's father had a winner with his Mongolian pony called Heathfield in the Tientsin Maidens, the Chinese couple took me for lunch where I could sample the famous Tientsin Dumplings. They looked after me for the first twenty-four hours; then I was on my own as they had to work. I was left at my hotel with nothing to do, so I decided to go to a video shop and buy a film in English as there was nothing I could watch on TV. I asked at the reception desk for written instructions I could give the taxi driver and ventured forth. I managed to find something I could watch and then set off to walk to the hotel. I asked the way as I could say the name of the hotel and, later, when lost again, the same person saw me and came up to help me. I felt completely safe in this city that saw very few foreigners in the early 2000s. The next day, on leaving the hotel by taxi in pouring rain, arriving at the railway station and having to manage my luggage going down an escalator, help appeared at once. The Chinese look after elderly foreigners, I discovered. I felt so safe, even though I did not come across anyone who spoke English.

The fifth trip I have selected from my many travels is my holiday to Australia in 2016. I was invited by a couple Val and I had met earlier that year on a cruise from Valparaiso to Buenos Aires. I had been to Australia several times, staying in Sydney in 1968 with friends, when we lived in Hong Kong. I had stayed in Perth in 2013, when it is unbearably hot, with Dick's cousin Christine and her husband Con. They had been most kind and hospitable and took me to Margaret River, to the wine growing area and the prison at Fremantle. We enjoyed a family get together in the Botanical Gardens in Perth. I had previously met one of Christine and Con's daughters in London, a second cousin to my sons. From there I had travelled on to Adelaide and then to Sydney, to stay with to stay with old Hong Kong friends in both places.

This time I flew direct to Perth from Hong Kong to stay with Roz and Terry Byelund. It was October, springtime in the southern hemisphere. They took me on a five-day trip north of Perth. It was my first time in the Outback, the Australian desert where I would see an abundance of wildflowers. It was unforgettable. We drove for two hours from Perth to our first stop, the Pinnacles. It is a sacred place for the local tribe with its stunning, natural limestone structures formed 25,000 –30,000 years ago after the sea receded. We went on to

Geraldton and the Kalgoorlie National Park, staying in very primitive accommodation (by European and the rest of Australia's standards) and it was all hugely enjoyable. Finally, we went to the Benedictine monastery at New Norsia. This was particularly special as Roddy Leece, our rector in my parish of St George's, Hanover Square, had stayed there and written a Mass setting. There is so much more I could say about the five-day trip with Roz and Terry. It made a lasting impression on me. I knew I had to go back, which I did the following year, and this time they took me down south to Albany.

In the difficult days after Dick's death, I could never have imagined having such bold adventures in such far-flung places around the globe. It is some consolation to know that he would have been hugely proud of me for showing such courage and perseverance. My mother gave up on life when my father retired and then died. I am proud of myself that I did not do the same.

CHAPTER 21: MENETS
AND CAZENOVES
Refugees and Bankers

I mentioned in the Introduction how I knew, from the family tree that Uncle Harold compiled, that my great-grandmother Emma Menet (1821–1902), who married Thomas Charrington (1819–1894) in 1845, was 'of Huguenot ancestry', but that was all I knew. It was through Debby's fantastic research skills that I discovered much about my Huguenot ancestors. I also learnt a great deal about the terrible persecution they faced in France, how they showed extraordinary resilience and, later, became hugely wealthy and successful in London. I even made a trip to France to explore the places associated with them, as I describe in the next chapter.

The term 'gateway ancestor' is particularly appropriate for Emma. It is notable that her lifespan was very similar to that of Queen Victoria (1819–1901). Debby discovered that she was baptised in the church of St John-at-Hackney on 25 May 1821. This was the same church the Charringtons attended and where she later married Thomas. Emma's parents, my great-great-grandparents John Francis Menet (1777-1835) and Louise Cazenove (1785-1871) were both of Huguenot stock. In this chapter, I shall first describe the origins of the Huguenot struggle in France and then I shall share what Debby discovered about John Francis' family, the Menets, and Louise's father's side, the Cazenoves. In Chapter 23 I shall continue with my Huguenot family tree, sharing the fascinating history of the Dalbiacs, Lamottes and Du Boulays, all ancestors on Louise Cazenove's mother's side.

Until I started to delve into my family history, I must confess to total ignorance of the Huguenot struggle in France. I did my best to find out what I could. On one occasion, I even drove to Rochester to hear Robin Gwynn lecture on

'Extremes of poverty and wealth among Huguenot refugees'. Sadly, I missed his talk at the Huguenot Museum there because I ignored the satnav and got lost. Notwithstanding this, I did learn something about the Huguenots, including the significance of the Edict of Nantes, proclaimed in 1598. Prior to then, France had been plagued by religious wars and the Calvinist Protestants of France, also known as 'the Huguenots', had suffered particularly badly, especially during the St Bartholomew's Day massacre which began on the night of 23/24 August 1572. Melvyn Bragg recounts, 'The River Seine ran red with Protestant blood.' There were seven Dalbiac families in Paris that night. Four of them were wiped out.

The fortunes of the Huguenots changed after Henry IV of France (1553–1610) came to the throne in 1589. He was baptised Catholic, but his mother brought him up Protestant. To secure the throne and promote national unity he converted to Catholicism and came out with the phrase 'Paris is worth a Mass.' However, he did sign the Edict of Nantes, which gave the Huguenots some substantial protection, allowing them to worship as they pleased, work more freely and bring grievances to the King.

In 1685, Henry's grandson, King Louis XIV (1638–1715), revoked the Edict of Nantes. He declared Protestantism illegal. Protestant ministers were given two weeks to leave the country unless they converted to Catholicism. They were then prohibited from leaving the country and another period of persecution began. The King's dragoons were sent through France to persuade the Huguenots to convert to the Catholic faith. The troops forcibly lodged in Huguenot homes where they looted and mistreated the inhabitants until they renounced their faith. Many Huguenots fled France to seek asylum in Geneva during this period. Indeed, many had already made their way to Geneva – the home of John Calvin - since 1523 and especially since the Bartholomew's Day Massacre back in 1572. It was a French-speaking city, which made it easy for refugees from France to assimilate.

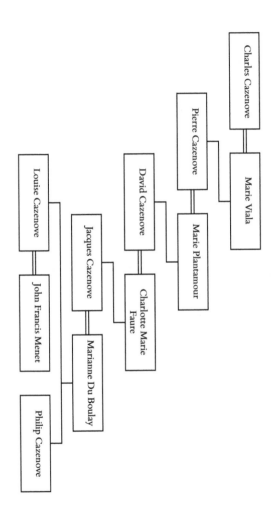

Descendent chart for Charles Cazenove.

Many Huguenots, including some of my ancestors, used Geneva as a midway point before proceeding to other European cities such as Amsterdam and London. One such family was the Menets. Their origins lie in Royas, near Beauchastel in the Vivarais region of France. They were a staunchly Protestant family and they fled France in the aftermath of the revocation of the Edict of Nantes. Some went to Turin; others, including my ancestor François Menet, went to Geneva. They set up a silk manufacturing company there. Francois's sister, Isabeau Fiales (née Menet) had been arrested with her husband whilst at a church service in France. Isabeau's husband was sent to the galleys for life and Isabeau herself was imprisoned for fifteen years in the Tour de Constance at Aigues-Mortes, a prison for heretic women, following a short spell in the Citadel du St Esprit. She was in fact only released because she had lost her mind. She was released to her family in 1750, her husband having died in Marseille, still in captivity, in 1742. Their little boy, Michel Ange, who was born in captivity, in the Citadel of St Esprit, and who had entered the Tour de Constance with his mother at the age of three months, was sent to live with other family members when he was six.

One of François Menet's descendants was my third-great-grandfather, Francis Menet, who married my third-great-grandmother Jeanne-Marguérite Auriol (also known as Jane). It is unclear when or where Francis was born, but Jeanne-Margaret was born in 1747, the daughter of my fourth-great-grandparents Elisée d'Auriol (1691–1778) and Marguérite de Bonnal. It seems from Elisée's will that his daughter married Francis Menet 'without his consent and against his advice'. Elisée did leave her money – and a lot of it – but it was under condition that Francis never got his hands on it. She survived Francis by many years and was buried in St Mary's, Islington (like some of the Newmans). It is not clear why Elisée did not like Francis, who was from a perfectly respectable Huguenot family, like theirs. Maybe he thought she

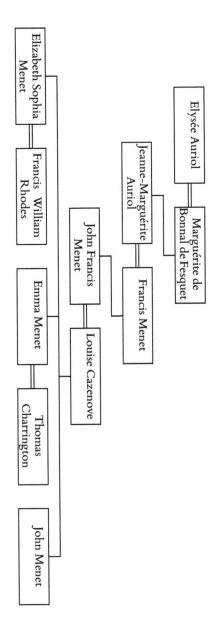

Descendant chart for Elysée Auriol.

could have done better for herself. After all, her sister married a Count and her mother, my fifth-great-grandmother Marguérite de Bonnal was the daughter of a Marquis. Indeed, it looks as if Francis and Jeanne-Marguérite eloped; they were married in 1775 at St John's in Margate. Francis became a silk merchant and traded in Old Broad Street, at number 80. An advertisement which appeared in the *Public Ledger and Daily Advertiser* of 6 March 1817 sheds some light on the family circumstances and the style in which the Menets lived:

> Spacious warehouse, dwelling house and premises in Old Broad Street and houses in White Lion Court. By Messrs Hoggart and Phillips. At Auction Mart near the Bank of England.

> The unexpired term in the lease of an excellent family house, in complete repair, containing numerous rooms of good proportions, cellaring, a large yard, warehouses and counting houses, in the occupation of Messrs Francis Menet and co., with a communication into White Lion Court, Throgmorton Street. Also, the lease for twenty-six years of two houses adjoining, numbers 2 and 3 White Lion Court, let for seventeen years at an improved rent of £8 per annum.

Francis and Jeanne-Marguérite's son, my great-great grandfather, John Francis Menet (1777-1835) was baptised in May 1777, at around one month old, in the Chapel of the Hospital, Spitalfields. His godparents were Elizabeth Devismes (his aunt had married into the noble Devismes family) and François Menet of Turin, presumably his father's cousin. The next we know is that the *Morning Post* of 30 July 1805 reported on the marriage on 29 July at St Mary's, Walthamstow, of John Francis Menet of Old Broad Street and Louise Cazenove, daughter of James Cazenove 'of Walthamstow'.

Louise's father, my third-great-grandfather James, also descended from a Huguenot family who had fled France for Geneva. The Cazenoves originated in Guienne, in the Aquitaine, near Bordeaux – as de Cazenove. However, my branch broke away, became Protestant, and one of my ancestors dropped the aristocratic 'de' and went into business as a silk merchant, settling in Anduze, in the Cévennes region of France from the 16th Century. Why did they choose Anduze? It had been for several centuries the centre of the silk trade in France, but it had also become the centre for Protestant resistance in the Cévennes. The Protestant community had their own Temple to worship in and they were probably reassured by a large city wall (although that was later destroyed during fighting and only the clock tower still stands). Following the Edict of Nantes, the community gained tolerance, at least for a while.

Pierre Cazenove, my fifth-great-grandfather, was born in Anduze, in relatively peaceful times, on 28 August 1670, one of seven children of my sixth-great-grandparents Charles Cazenove (b.1634) and Maria Viala. Family records written by Pierre indicate that Charles married Maria on 1 December 1666. When Pierre was a few months short of his fifteenth birthday, Louis XIV revoked the Edict of Nantes and intense persecution of Protestants began again.

Enough was enough. The family was becoming impoverished, and they were now in real danger. Pierre set off for Geneva with his nine-year-old brother, Charles. We have no historical records for what happened to Pierre's parents. There were family legends which suggest the boys arrived with virtually no money or means of support. In Geneva, they met a draper by the name of Jean Plantamour who took Pierre on as an apprentice. Pierre married Jean's daughter Marie on 15 June 1697 at the Temple de la Madeleine, still standing today in Rue de Toutes Ames. The Plantamour family originated in Chalon-sur-Saône, eastern France. Jean Plantamour, and his brother Philippe fled as refugees to Geneva where they established a successful cloth business. There is a Rue Philippe Plantamour in Geneva, named after a later descendant. Pierre's marriage to my fifth-great-grandmother Maria was regarded as a very beneficial one; it gave him an immediate entrée into Genevan society and enabled him to set up in business himself. It also gave him that all-important reach into Amsterdam, which allowed the Cazenoves to become merchant bankers, not simply merchants. Pierre was admitted to the *bourgeoisie* of Geneva in 1703.

Pierre and Maria had four sons. The youngest was my fourth-great-grandfather David Cazenove (1711–1782). He was born in Geneva and married twice. Both wives had the same first name: Charlotte Bectel and, my fourth-great-grandmother Charlotte Faure (1720–1781), whom he married in 1737. David's son, my third-great-grandfather Jacques Cazenove (b.1744) changed his name to James when he became the first Cazenove to arrive in London. Two of his brothers, Charles and John, made their way to London also. The Cazenove business in Geneva had close links with the East India company. The family were then established in London by about 1775 and James set up business as a merchant, also with a counting-house in Old Broad Street. James married my third-great-grandmother Marianne du Boulay (1761–1849), about whose ancestry we shall learn in Chapter 23.

James and Marianne had nine children – four boys and five girls. They started their married life in the City of London and some of the children were baptised in and around the City – first at the Artillery Church in Spitalfields and then at St Martin Orgar in Eastcheap. Their daughter Louise Cazenove, my great-great-grandmother, was born on 29 January 1785 and baptised at home on Saturday 26 February, by Pastor Jacob Bourdillon of the Artillery Church. Her godparents were her uncle François Houssemayne du Boulay and Louise du Boulay, her grandmother. In 1792, when Marianne's grandfather, Jean Lagier Lamotte (1708–1792), died, James was mentioned in the will as living in Martin Lane, Cannon Street. By about 1799, the family was living in Upper Clapton and worshipping at the church of St John-at-Hackney. Their last few years were spent in Hornsey and there is a family vault at St Mary's Church in Hornsey where they and various other family members are buried. James died in 1827 and Marianne in 1849.

The annual register states that James died in his eighty-third year at his residence in Crouch End, formerly a merchant of great respectability in Old Broad Street.

As mentioned above, Louise married my great-great-grand-father, John Francis Menet in Walthamstow in 1805. John Francis Menet became a stockbroker with a business already established in London and his brother-in-law, Philippe Cazenove, joined forces with him. Philip and his brothers were educated at Charterhouse School. He married Emma Knapp in 1822; his old Charterhouse headmaster John Russell officiated at the ceremony. When Philip died in 1880, he was described as 'one of the few of London's merchant princes who gave, as God had blessed them, to the Church and to the poor'. Another of the Cazenove brothers, John, became a businessman and political economist and a friend and supporter of Robert Malthus.

After their marriage, John Francis and Louise lived in Shacklewell, now part of Dalston, but then very much a village. 'Gentlemen' apparently lived in houses on both sides of Shacklewell Lane. The Rhodes family were neighbours – they lived at Shacklewell Lodge. Much of the area was open country, used for market gardens, nurseries and pasture. Hackney had become a favoured spot for merchants. The area was changing; its proximity to the City made it increasingly popular. When their daughter, my great-grandmother Emma Menet, was five, John Francis took out a lease on Frognal Park in Hampstead, known to be the grandest house in the area. This was in 1826 and the Menets would have just taken over the lease when William Newman (Robert Finch Newman's brother mentioned in Chapter 9) committed suicide. Frognal was recognised for the 'salubrity of its air'. John Francis Menet died in 1835 at Hampstead, aged sixty-four. Louise continued to live at Frognal with her mother Marianne du Boulay until Emma married in 1845.

Emma had two sisters. The first was Mary Ann, born in 1807, who married Charles Vernet of Geneva and settled with him there. They had seven children. Mary died in 1847. It is through Mary that I am related to Prudence Glynn, Baroness Windlesham (1935–1986), the first fashion editor for *The Times*. The other sister was Elizabeth Sophia Menet, born in 1811. It was she who was the first wife of Francis William Rhodes. Elizabeth Sophia died in 1835, whereupon Francis re-married and fathered a son, the famous Cecil Rhodes. Emma also had a younger brother, John Menet, who became Vicar of All Saints, Hockerill and founded a teacher training college for ladies there. It still exists as a school, the Anglo-European College.

Louise sold the lease of Frognal following Emma's marriage and she went to live with her son John in Bishop's Stortford. She died there in 1871, in her eighty-seventh year and after a very long widowhood. Her Huguenot history on her father's side was just as rich on her mother's side, as we shall see in Chapter 23 – though not before I describe my journey to France where I was able to engage much more closely with this history myself.

CHAPTER 22: HUGUENOT TRAIL
The French Connection

I love to travel, and I was lucky to have a friend who, when I asked him if he would like to accompany me to France to learn more about my ancestors, agreed at once. So it was that, in March 2019, Hugh Priestley and I set off on our Huguenot trail.

We flew to Montpelier from Gatwick. It should have been Brexit Day and we decided, in case it made leaving the channel ports difficult, that we would fly and hire a car on arrival. This was the right decision, and it was all straightforward. Once Hugh adjusted to hugging the right side of the road – there were a few sharp intakes of breath on my part – he drove beautifully in a brand-new Ford Focus with brilliant satnav.

We managed to find our first hotel on the outskirts of Uzès and that was the only disappointment of our trip. The First Great Western there was not good. However, after a drink in the bar, we drove into the delightful town of Uzès. Described as 'a pretty, tucked away, almost secret, market town in the South of France' it was indeed a treasure and made me realise how much I adore France. With a good choice of Michelin-starred restaurants and easy parking, we had two *gastronomique* evenings. I loved the atmosphere of the first particularly, and we chose a bottle of Chateau de Cazeneuve which we thought a good start to our trip. It was delicious. In addition, the service was wonderful and the setting, in an old cattle market, was superb.

The next morning, we set off for Anduze: gateway to the Cévennes region and from where many Huguenots, including my Cazenove ancestors, fled France for Geneva. Anduze stretches between two mighty rock formations. What immediately struck me and caused me to fall in love with the town was that the backdrop of the mountains reminded me of the

Rawla Narlai in Rajasthan where I had spent two nights in January with a tour group. The River Gardon flows through Anduze, which was an important silk-trading centre from the Middle Ages. It is also famous for its Protestant history and its pottery workshops. Its central area includes the Grand Temple of Anduze where my ancestors would have worshipped.

We also went to the Musée du Désert in nearby Mialet with its fifteen rooms about Huguenot history. We were not disappointed. *Désert* means a secret and secluded location. We were in what was once a very important Protestant base chosen by the excluded population, made up of teachers, notaries, lawyers, and artisan clothworkers. They were literate people, and few peasant farmers joined them. The museum has a bookshop where I bought *Pages d'Histoire Protestant: L'Exode des Huguenots:* sixty-four pages of illustrations and accounts, with, fortunately, an English translation. The name of one of the female Protestants who had perished caught my eye: '1737 MENET Isabeau' – one of my relatives, my fifth-great-aunt. She was the sister of my fourth-great-grandfather François Menet and was arrested with her husband and her sister Jeanne on 1 July 1735 because they had been to a Protestant meeting held by Pasteur Pradon held on 29 March 1735. I mention in Chapter 21 how she was imprisoned and eventually became insane. I started to feel my search was coming alive.

We also visited Nîmes, the most Roman city outside Italy and the most Protestant in France.

The 'Michelade' is the name given to the massacre of Catholics here, including of twenty-four priests and monks, by Protestant rioters on 29 September 1567. We visited the Cathedral which documents the tumultuous history of Nîmes and to Place aux Herbes where the Michelade took place. I reveal more in Chapter 23 about how it was from Nîmes that my sixth-great-grandfather Jacques Dalbiac (1712–1792) fled to England. His noble family had been in Nîmes from 13th Century. Before that they were in Albi, the centre of the Cathar sect which was ruthlessly suppressed by Pope Innocent III.

Later that year, Hugh and I made a second trip to France. We travelled first to La Motte Chalancon. The drive from the Château de Rochegude was magnificent. We went through unlit rock tunnels and came out into the bright sunlight, with the rugged terrain of the gorge surrounding us. The rocks were mostly grey but red tinged in parts. We passed through a gorge and Hugh stopped the car once or twice so I could take photos, but I was disappointed my camera did not really capture the awesome scenery. La Motte Chalancon is a small town or *commune* surrounded by mountains in the Auvergne-Rhône-Alpes region of south-west France. It is an area favoured by campers. Debby put this on my list of 'must-sees' as it from here that Jacques's son-in-law, my fifth-great-grandfather Jean Lagier La Motte (1708-1792), fled from France to Geneva in 1694.

It was about noon on Monday 5 August – and market day – when we arrived in La Motte Chalancon. On the street by the market was a crowded café with everyone sitting outside. We could not face joining them due to the heat and wandered along past the market stalls to find shorts and a sun hat for me. One stall particularly caught my eye. On first sight I thought it was a display of cheeses, but on closer inspection I saw they were huge chunks of nougat. As I stood in the market, looking at the surrounding mountains, I wondered how on earth, in the late 17th Century, the Huguenots had managed to flee to Geneva. The fear of persecution or death at the hands of the Catholics, had caused thousands to take what must have been a perilous journey. It is nearly 300 km as the crow flies to Geneva, and I tried to imagine the treacherous route they must have taken over the Alps. I wonder how many days they took to reach Geneva. The guidebooks say that today it takes three and a half hours by car.

The next day we went to Le Poet-Laval to visit the Musée du Protestantisme Dauphinois. The museum was a disappointment compared to the Musée du Désert at Mialet, but the town was a gem. Le Poet-Laval is another commune. It is easily missed but when you eventually arrive it is worth getting lost in the attempt. Cars are not allowed in the picturesque village, so we parked below and walked up the main street where there was a restaurant. Madame told us that the museum was closed from 12 noon to 3 p.m. and so at 12.30 p.m. we sat down and ordered lunch. Even though the temperature was in the 30s we manage to enjoy the local dishes. Goats' cheese is renowned here, with pasta. The company of two delightful campers at the next table who come every year from Geneva and Marseilles added to our enjoyment. We exchanged emails, and both said they would come to London. As it was nearing 3 p.m., we found the car and drove up to the medieval castle and the museum. We stood on the side of a hill to get a breeze, until the museum opened. This probably started life as a residence of one of the Knights Hospitaller and then in the 15th Century became the village hall before being converted into a Protestant temple in 1622.

The curator spoke French too rapidly even for Hugh and I felt I did not get a lot out of the visit. We sat in the temple with two other tourists: its rough stone walls and plain wooden pulpit and gallery were a reminder of the contrast between Catholicism and Protestantism in that period of history.

However, exploring the castle and narrow streets made up for the disappointment of the museum itself. The defensive walls date back to the 14th Century and we wandered the narrow, cobbled streets delighting in the many perfect, picture-postcard views they afforded. Finally, we climbed the steps of the castle tower and were rewarded a great view of the village down below. Even the heat was not going to deter me. Le Poet-Laval is one of the most beautiful villages in the region.

The next morning, at breakfast, we talked to a French couple. By coincidence, Madame was a Huguenot from Anduze but had not heard of the Musée du Protestantisme at Le Poet-Laval.

Hugh and I also visited Arles and Lyon on this trip. In Lyon, we visited *les traboules* or the secret passageways of the city. Dating back to the 4th Century, they were built to allow more people direct access to fresh water than the winding streets provided. Jews hid in them during the Second World War, as did Huguenots in earlier centuries. Debby told me that my eighth-great-grandfather, Abraham Penin, a candlestick maker, had lived in the old part of the town with his wife Jeanne Pelloutier and their seven children. Jeanne and Abraham were both born a few years after the St Bartholomew Massacre (1572) The killing did not only take place in Paris; Protestants in Lyons were rounded up and taken to a prison to be killed. Perhaps my ancestors hid in the *traboules*. In less troubled times, Abraham was one of the church elders. There is a possible family connection, yet to be explored, between Jeanne and Abraham and Diana, Princess of Wales.

It was wonderful on my two trips to France to feel so much more connected to these ancestors who endured so much. I also had the added benefits of superb food, fine wine, and Hugh's wonderful company.

CHAPTER 23 : DALBIACS, LAMOTTES
AND DU BOULAYS
Merchants and Weavers

We have already explored the Huguenot history of my great-grandmother Emma Menet's on her father side (the Menets) and her mother's paternal side (the Cazenoves), but in this chapter we encounter more Huguenots on her mother's maternal side, namely the Dalbiacs, Lamottes and Du Boulays.

In the previous chapter, I briefly introduced the first of these, the Dalbiacs, as I visited where they lived prior to fleeing France. Unlike most of my Huguenot ancestors who fled to Geneva and then made their way to England, my Dalbiac (sometimes written D'Albiac) ancestors came direct to London. In 1685, my seventh-great-grandparents, Scipio Dalbiac and Marie Durand (b.1660) were living in Nîmes when the Edict of Nantes was revoked. The story is that, whereas an uncle converted to Catholicism to save the family estate, Marie and her three daughters refused to convert and were murdered. Their two sons Scipio (later known as Simon) and Jacques escaped, as they were looked after by the family maid, who was a Catholic. She hid them successfully and then took them to Calais. She put them in the custody of an English lady travelling to London, hiding them amongst her linen, who then handed them over to the Huguenot community in Spitalfields. They were taken in by a Madame Caduc, who had a weaving business and lived in Spital Square on the eastern edge of the City of London. Apparently, two little caps worn by the boys survived and were handed down the family for several generations. Jacques Dalbiac (later known as James), my sixth-great-grandfather, was four years old when he arrived in London.

James Dalbiac – also known as Captain James Dalbiac – became a master weaver and he settled in Spitalfields; he was

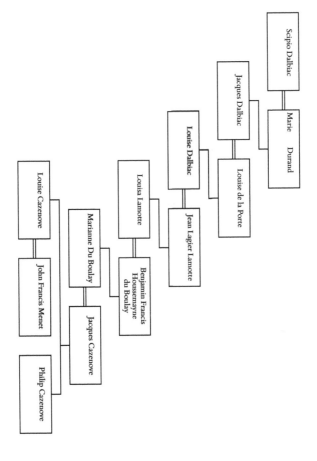

Descendant chart for Scipio Dalbiac.

admitted to the Weavers' Company as a Foreign Weaver in 1711. His first premises were in Brick Lane. He concentrated his business on silk and velvet and 'the black branch' of the silk industry – this being mourning attire. He seized the chance to cash in on the increase in public mourning and more ostentatious funerals.

In 1710, he married my sixth-great-grandmother, Louise Delaporte, in the Liberty of Norton Folgate. Louise's father, Charles Delaporte, was also a Master Weaver based in the Low Leyton area who came originally from the Cévennes in France. Her mother, another Louise, was originally from Niort. In 1712, Louise gave birth to yet another Louise, my fifth-great-grandmother, Louise Dalbiac (1712–1792), who was baptised at the Artillery Church in Spitalfields. Her godparents were her uncle Scipio and Louise (also known as Lucy) Delaporte (*née* Plumail), her maternal grandmother.

James and Louise settled in Spital Square, first at no. 7. This would have been quite a step-up from their previous accommodation in Brick Lane. However, all the windows in his house were broken in 1720 by rioting journeymen weavers, during the anti-calico campaign. They very nearly wrecked the house. The journeymen alleged that James had called them lazy and work-shy. There was considerable unemployment at the time, thought by the silk industry to be due to the increasing use and wear of printed calicoes instead of silks. James denied having said anything of the sort. It must have been very frightening for the family.

They moved to No. 20 Spital Square, an even grander house, by about 1727. In 1745, James offered a large contingent of men – eighty of his workmen - to resist the Young Pretender. When he died in 1749, he was described as 'an eminent black silk weaver reputed to have died very rich' When his wife Louise died in 1776, she left a considerable amount of money to the French Protestant Church and to the French charity school in Windmill Street. I was delighted to visit

James Dalbiac, his wife Louise (*née* Delaporte) and their five children.

Spitalfields with Steven Saxby and explore the old Huguenot quarter. Some of the houses there have been preserved as they were in the 18th century. We also visited Denis Severs's House in Folgate Street, a recreation of what such a house would have looked, sounded and smelt like at the time my ancestors lived there.

In 1734, Louise Dalbiac married my fifth-great-grandfather, Jean Lagier Lamotte (1708–1792). The ceremony was at the church of St Martin Orgar, which used to stand in Martin Lane, off Cannon Street and was then being used by a French Protestant congregation. Jean was described as 'of the parish of St Bartholomew' and Louise as being resident within the parish of St Martin Orgar. Witnesses were Daniel Lagier Lamotte, Jean's brother, and Simon Dalbiac, perhaps Louise's brother. Jean Lagier Lamotte was born in 1708 and baptised at the Temple of the Madeleine in Geneva, the son of my sixth-great-grandparents Claude Lagier Lamotte and his wife Marie. He had a brother, Daniel. Both brothers came to England and were naturalised as British citizens, Jean in 1732. The

Lamottes were originally from the Dauphin area of France. Jean became a merchant with premises at Bishopsgate. There is a deed dated 1774 in the Essex Archives relating to the refinancing by Augustine Gwyn of his purchase of the Mount Charles plantation in Jamaica. Jean was one of the investors.

Jean and Louise had several children including another Louise, my fourth-great-grandmother Louise Lamotte (1736–1825). Church records show that she was born on 10 May 1736 and baptised at the French Hospital Chapel in Spitalfields. Her godparents were her uncle, Daniel Lagier Lamotte, and her grandmother, also Louise Dalbiac, née Louise de la Porte. Jean and Louise both died in 1792 – Jean in late September and Louise in February. Both were buried at the church of St Mary the Virgin in Wanstead. In his will, Jean expressed the hope that his body should be interred no more than five days after his death, in the most decent and least expensive way, with only one hearse, a mourning coach and a pair of horses in attendance. Jean's will mentions the interest in the Mount Charles plantation and certain estates on the Island of St Christopher (now better known as St Kitts). These seem to have passed down the line of his son and namesake, Jean Lagier Lamotte, although he made sure his daughter Louise was well-provided for. Her son-in-law, James Cazenove, who we encountered in Chapter 21, was one of the executors.

Louise Lamotte married in 1756 at St Martin Outwich, which was used by Huguenots and used to stand near Threadneedle Street before it was demolished in 1874. She married my fourth-great-grandfather Benjamin Francis du Boulay (1725-1765). He was born in Île de la France, Paris, the son of my fifth-great-grandparents Francois du Boulay and a Mademoiselle Devismes. When Debby first told me about him, the name du Boulay struck a chord. On a cruise a couple of years ago, I met Anthony du Boulay, a ceramics expert and writer. I fell for his charm, energy and exuberance. At the age of 90 he surpassed many men far younger. Like Hugh Priestley, who was with me on the cruise, he was a 'Wykehamist', a former pupil of Winchester College, one of the oldest independent boarding schools for boys. Our common ancestors, the du Boulay family, were also Huguenot refugees, who fled to Holland after the Revocation. They took little with them in their flight; only a silver seal which established their connection with the Marquis d'Argenson, a prominent family of French politicians. .

Benjamin went on to study theology at the University of Leiden. He qualified as a minister and first went to Amsterdam before he was invited by the elders of the French church in Threadneedle Street, often known as 'Geneva on Threadneedle Street', to serve as their pastor in London. He was the fifth pastor to have been appointed. At some point, he changed his name from 'du Boulay' to 'Houssemayne du Boulay'. He was ordained in the Temple Church by Thomas Sherlock, bishop of London, first as deacon in 1751 and then as priest in 1753. After he married Louise, they lived with his growing family in Fournier Street (at no. 12), which is one of those preserved streets in Spitalfields I visited with Steven. He died in 1765, only in his forties, and was buried at the Huguenot church in Southampton, St Julien's, which is still standing. Louise was left with five children under the age of eight. They were taken in by relatives at Wanstead. When she died in 1825, she requested in her will that she be buried 'in as plain a manner as possible'. She was laid to rest in the Cazenove family vault in Hornsey.

One of Benjamin and Louise's five children was my third-great-grandmother Marianne du Boulay (1761–1849) who married Jacques (or James) Cazenove (b.1744) on 18 January 1781 in Wanstead. Records show that Marianne was baptised on 6 December 1761 at the French Hospital Chapel in Spitalfields, having been born on 17 November 1761. Her older brother, Francis Houssemayne du Boulay (1759-1728), became a financier and stock jobber. He left a fortune worth nearly

£28 million in today's money when he died. He owned the house in Walthamstow, known as 'Forest' which became the Forest School, where my grandfather, Francis Charrington, was educated. We already saw in Chapter 21 that Marianne and James' daughter, Louise Cazenove (b.1785), married Jean Francis Menet (1777–1835) and that their daughter, born with such extraordinary Huguenot heritage, was my great-grandmother, Emma Menet, the mother of Francis Charrington (1858–1947). Emma was the 'gateway ancestor' through which Debby and I discovered so much about my Huguenot ancestors. I am full of admiration for all they achieved. Even from such horrifying circumstances, they found a way.

CONCLUSION:
Finding a Way

The night I met Dick on 15 August 1962, when he took me to a nightclub in Mayfair, was over half a century ago; now I am living in a flat in Bourdon Street, just around the corner from the Blue Angel where we had our first dance. Dick's stepmother Marjorie urged us to go and see the flat in the early 1970s, as her sister Nina wanted to move and hence stop leasing the flat from the Grosvenor Estate. We fell in love with it at once. It is a first and second floor maisonette with a garage, in a quiet street, higgledy-piggledy with stairs up and down and an outside space at the back. The houses on the right-hand side of the street as you walk down, are late 19th-century mews houses. The grooms from the big houses in Berkeley and Grosvenor Squares kept their horses in what are now the garages.

It was our second home from 1974 to 2004, and then we moved here from Island Farm permanently when Dick was no longer allowed to drive. It became increasingly difficult to leave him and I wanted to continue in my profession as a Jungian psychologist in London, working from the flat in Mayfair. It was becoming too difficult to leave Dick alone in Kent. We went, therefore, through one of the most traumatic experiences in life: packing up and leaving a much-loved family home. We had lived there for thirty-four years, all the time since leaving Hong Kong in 1969 except for the first six months after our return to England.

At first it was difficult to adjust to living in a much smaller space, and our packing cases took up most of the sitting room. A wonderful neighbour, Robin, helped me unpack, for which I remain eternally grateful. Within days of our arrival, I saw wooden hoardings being erected next door. I had a sense of dread because I discovered that three houses next door were going to be knocked into one and that the developers were excavating for a swimming pool in the basement. I knew this would cause us enormous disruption. It endorsed my feeling of helplessness in the face of the richest landlords in the country, the Grosvenor Estate owned by the Duke of Westminster. For the entire time leading up to Dick's death, and afterwards, we had to endure drilling, banging, damp coming in from next door, noise, and disruption. I was so stressed that I ceased to realise the impact it was having on us. Sarah, the PA to the CEO of the Grosvenor Estate, advised me to take photos and send them to Grosvenor. She used the garage in the street to park her car and could see what we were having to endure. I did write and the day before Dick's funeral they managed to clean up the front door of 30a, which by then was exposed and which looked filthy. Later, Grosvenor went much further than this. Within two months of Dick's death, I received a phone call. Unofficially it was suggested I asked for compensation. The property developer who was responsible had not stuck to his contract of finishing his building project by mid-July, so I was able to ask for a year's refund on rent. I was being heard, despite feeling like a voice in the wilderness. It made a difference, but I was a long way off from building up my self-confidence after all I had been through. During that challenging time, walking in Hyde Park in the lovely September sunshine with our yellow Labrador kept me sane. Later, one of my daughters-in-law, Lisa, designed our outside space for us, so now I have a small but delightful garden. Despite the challenges when we first made Mayfair our permanent home, Dick felt settled here and, after only two months, we abandoned the idea of buying the long lease from Grosvenor and selling it to move somewhere larger with a garden. We decided to stay on as 'protected' or 'statutory' tenants. Dick died three years later.

Following Dick's death, I have been on my own for nearly fourteen years and have gradually come to feel part of the furniture, or fabric, of Mayfair. It took a while, as I was looking

after Dick, working as a psychologist, and felt generally un-
sure of myself. My first local connection was with Grosvenor
Chapel. Dick and I started attending shortly after we moved
from Kent. The priest, Father Simon Hobbs, was a great
source of comfort and support leading up to and after Dick's
death. There were some great people in the congregation and
my social life revolved around them for the first year. I now
attend St George's, Hanover Square, and our rector, Roddy
Leece, is a joy in every way. I have so enjoyed his monthly
'Holy Cocktails', drinks with a great mix of people, and, more
recently, the 'Rector's Rambles', local walks on Fridays which
are informative and fun.

I became interested in local politics when Dick and I first
moved here permanently in 2004. I joined the committee of
the West End Ward of the Conservatives. It was a rocky ride
for many years with people who were unsuitable to take office - many ups and downs and much in-fighting. There were
warring factions, which did not make an easy ride. However, we managed to organise one or two excellent fund-raising
events, both attended by the then Home Secretary, Theresa
May, at the home of our Chairman, Jonathan Glanz. We also
hosted Amber Rudd at the Lansdowne Club. Amber was delightful, warm and friendly as opposed to Theresa May's cold-
ness. She spotted I had invited a table of friends, as opposed to
strangers, to fill a table: very observant, I thought. Sadly, two
of our councillors were de-selected before the local elections
of Spring 2018, which meant Labour got a foothold before we
could start canvassing. We now have a Labour councillor Pan-
cho Lewis and two Conservative, Jonathan Glanz, the current
Lord Mayor of Westminster, and Timothy Barnes, as well as
a new MP who was formerly Leader of the Council, Nickie
Aiken. She is great. Since I joined the West End ward of the
Conservative Party, I have been on the committee. In fact,
I have served as Vice Chairman, and I am now the Deputy
Chairman.

I also learned to play bridge and have been playing now for several years. I joined the Lansdowne Club, which is a five-minute walk away, and which I use for swimming. Three years ago, I was persuaded by a friend and neighbour, Lucy, to be a Residents Representative on the Steering Committee the Mayfair Neighbourhood Forum. I was not at all confident that I would succeed in getting enough votes, but Lucy insisted I would. 'You know everybody,' she said. I was duly elected. I realised various friends, old and new, helped me to get through the re-building my life. If it had not been for Lucy, I would never have had put myself up to be a residents rep. I messaged Lucy recently to thank her for pushing me forward. It has made a difference to my life in Mayfair. I am no longer intimidated by the 'big boys'; I have friends who believe in me.

So, gradually, I found my feet, but it was not easy. At first, I was very aware that I was without the back-up of a one-time successful husband and a lovely home in the country. I was widowed, and my sons all married with children and their own interests. My neighbours were a lot younger, and I did not want to be a burden to them. It was a stark discovery to find I was no longer the centre of anyone's life. I was, however, beginning to find my own way. When our beautiful Labrador, Jasper, died, I decided not to get another dog even though I missed him terribly. At one point, several years after Dick's death, I wanted to find a partner as the prospect of living on my own for the rest of my life frightened me. I even registered with a very expensive dating agency. It was not a success and I realised I was better off on my own. I was young for my age and the agency only put me in touch with men who seemed old, tired, and disinterested, or else eager to have someone to look after them. This was not what I wanted. I decided it was better to stick with the friends I have who love and appreciate me. I was also loving being able to travel to places I had never

My MA graduation ceremony.

been before. Why give up this independence which I had for the first time in my life?

In July 2008, exactly a year after Dick died, I attended a writing course, which led to me then studying for an MA in Creative Non-Fiction Writing at City University. I had been enthusiastic about this course since I had attended an Arvon writing course in Devon the previous July on 'Life Writing'. Julie Wheelwright had been one of the tutors at Totleigh Barton, near Tavistock, and let it be known she had recently started this course at City. Once enrolled, we were required to write a biography or memoir. After my MA, I would not say I was brimming over with confidence, but with the help of Peter Moore, published author of several non-fiction books, and on the course before me, I managed to get my book about Dick, *All I Ever Wanted,* into good enough shape to send to an editor, my friend in Hong Kong, Carol Dyer. It was duly published, and I had a book launch at Grosvenor Chapel. After this, I was free to enjoy more travelling with my sister-in-law Val Charrington. We went to Vietnam, Hong Kong and on a cruise from Valparaiso to Buenos Aires. I have also enjoyed many weekends away in Kent with old friends Sue and Chris Boyd, Diana and Peter Wiggins, and Jenny and Robin Tait. These did much to restore my morale.

One of my favourite holidays in recent years was my time in Northern California with Robin Newton, where, as I mentioned in the Introduction, I began to write this book. Before this Robin had visited me in London. She was on a business trip and we had an action-packed weekend: including *Swan Lake* at the Royal Opera House, Covent Garden, with dinner in the Crush Room. A friend managed to obtain the tickets for us, and my favourite solo dancer in the role of Odile/Odette was Marianela Núñez. It was a perfect evening. The next day we had a River Thames boat cruise and dinner out in Piccadilly. On the Sunday we drove down to Rye, East Sussex to show Robin the picturesque Cinque Port. She was not disappointed. The narrow, cobbled streets, once the centre for smuggling when Rye was by the sea, make it a top tourist destination. She loved the Mermaid Inn. We went on to my youngest son James and his family near Goudhurst in Kent for a champagne and cream tea. This made it the perfect weekend for my dear friend from California. She had loved James as a baby in Hong Kong in 1968 and now here he was with his wife Jane and four children in a lovely Kentish farmhouse set in three acres of garden. It was good to be with Robin again the following October when I started to write this book among the Redwoods.

When I returned to Mayfair from America, buildings were being pulled down and new ones were being erected. Many of my neighbours are foreign millionaires I have never met. There are constant refurbishments every time a new owner takes possession. When I consider this, I wonder why I live here. My street is mixed, full of contrasts - mews houses and social housing - and I think this mix is probably what keeps me sane and not particularly concerned that I never meet the lady next door, who is said to be from Oman. Representing the residents on the local Forum creates a balance for me and makes me feel part of the community, so I can know what is going on in the ever-changing West End of London. My middle son Matthew told me that it is better to be relevant where I am, rather than the opposite in the country. I am an eighty-something extrovert and still have the desire to travel: 'Globe-trotting Grandma' is a nickname I have been given by my two eldest grandsons; I do not want to know about the less flattering ones.

On her visit to London, Robin told me she had met someone and was planning to get married. Since her divorce ten years ago, Robin had worked extremely hard to keep the family home going. I was so delighted to hear she had met a wonderful man online and so made a huge effort to attend her wedding early in March 2020. I decided, foolhardy in the opinions of three close friends who advised me against going, to leave on March 10 for San Jose. On arrival at the airport Robin was there to meet me with her two daughters. The sun was shining and, as I had travelled business class, I did not feel too bad. We arrived at the beautiful Los Altos house that Jim, Robin's fiancé, had rented, and I realised at once how Robin's life had changed: it was much grander than the small apartment where she had lived with her two daughters and son, along with Archie the Corgi and their ginger cat.

Soon after my return, our lives changed very promptly. The first inkling I had of Covid-19 was my awareness of what was happening when I was in Sri Lanka at the end of January. I saw pictures on *The Times* online of the deserted streets of Wuhan, China due to an epidemic. I dismissed the whole thing as something that might happen in China, in a city I had never heard of, but never to us, here in Britain. How wrong I was. I returned from the wedding in California on 18 March and duly went into quarantine followed by the lockdown on

23 March 2020, which was for everyone. It came as a horrible shock to realise I could not stay with my family, even for a birthday picnic outside. I tried booking a cottage in Kent, but it simply was not possible. So, I had to adjust to the fact I was going to spend Easter and my 84th birthday alone. There would be Zoom family calls, and Facetime. It was difficult to sleep at night, and impossible to settle down to anything. Every day was the same with no pressure to perform the simplest of tasks. I thought, at least, I would be able to write.

At first, I found it difficult to settle down to write. I noticed things that had changed in the last year. Our street, with its mix of mews houses and social housing is no longer as harmonious as it used to be. The rubbish situation is dire and the former, responsible behaviour of residents has all but disappeared. Laziness is prevalent and people do not seem to care anymore. To add to this, we had a crime scene last summer - with a stabbing! Two residents from social housing were having a drug-related fight; one stabbed the other. I dialled 999 and a dozen police arrived on the scene. One of them remarked to me, 'But this is Mayfair!'

It may be strange, but it is home, and it is here I have reflected deeply on how my family research has taken me on many journeys, not only to other parts of London, England, and the world, but through journeys of self-discovery. I have had to stay home for much of the pandemic but fortunately was able to form a temporary bubble at Christmas and celebrate with my son James and his family. When back in Mayfair I spent some time with Matthew's family on Zoom. We played 'Tree-Flower-Bird'. I did not think I stood much chance with my eldest grandson, Jamie, now a Master of Science, but I did not do too badly. I thought I had beaten him, but when they went through the scores later, they decided I had cheated. Mayfair was a sad place during the three lockdowns, with all non-essential shops closed. Pubs and restaurants, theatres, cinemas and museums, and most churches were closed also. I am

Diana with Trigger.

delighted mine stayed open and we could pray in the church building as the West End of London, which of course includes

Mayfair, started to come alive again. I was fully vaccinated but with nowhere to go. It is such a relief that things seem to be getting back to normal.

Writing this book was life-enhancing to me during the year of the depressing pandemic. It has given me focus and a purpose. In such challenging times it is easy to lose one's way. It was good to reflect deeply on my ancestry. I am an extrovert, normally always on the go and spending time with others. The pandemic made me slow down and gave me to time to think. It was so fascinating to delve into the stories of my ancestors and to think about how they have contributed to me being the person I am today. I was able to apply some of my Jungian skills and insights from astrology to consider the personalities of people who were otherwise just names on Uncle Harold's tree. Through Debby's research I discovered that my ancestry is so much more interesting and diverse than I could ever have imagined. Through my visits to places associated with my ancestors, especially in London, I now feel more connected to the city in which I live. Most importantly, I was able to reflect in detail on my own life, about the many experiences I have had, and how I have indeed taken every opportunity to find a way.

Ready for the next adventure.

Lightning Source UK Ltd.
Milton Keynes UK
UKHW022223140521
383738UK00007B/319